"What an extraordinary bond these women have forged as they worked on this book, and what an overwhelming sense of trust each must have placed in the other to attempt it. *Shallow Graves* is more than an act of collaboration; it is the work of two women who have achieved a state of sympathy, a harmony of minds, that most people seek but never achieve."
                                        —Douglas Balz, *Chicago Tribune*

"*Shallow Graves* is remarkable. There is nothing like it in print."
                                        —Ward Just, novelist and former
                                        Washington Post correspondent in Vietnam

"*Shallow Graves* is proving a fabulous success. Once into it, I read it straight through the night."
                                        —Beverley Jackson, *Santa Barbara News Press*

"For all the preoccupation with Vietnam, Americans paid surprisingly little attention to the people among whom we fought. *Shallow Graves* . . . opens a window on who the Vietnamese were and what happened to them. In doing so, it also helps us explain what happened to us."
                                        — Arnold P. Isaacs, *Atlanta Constitution*

"Wrenching to read . . . A comparatively understated and reflective book . . . Generates a special force in the context of what has been told in more conventional memoirs."
                                        —Bob Halliday, *Washington Post Book World*

"Surprisingly lovely . . . *Shallow Graves* offers an evocative personal look at a turbulent time."
                                        —Mary Vespa, *People*

the Intimate man

JAMES E. KILGORE

Abingdon Press
Nashville

The Intimate Man

Copyright © 1984 by Abingdon Press

Library of Congress Cataloging in Publication Data
KILGORE, JAMES E.
    The intimate man.
    1. Men—Psychology. 2. Intimacy (Psychology)
3. Interpersonal Relations. I. Title.
HQ1090.K54   1984   305.3   83-15908

ISBN 0-687-19128-9 (soft)

MANUFACTURED BY THE PARTHENON PRESS AT
NASHVILLE, TENNESSEE, UNITED STATES OF AMERICA

for
My sons Jim and Jeff—
two intimate men
in process

Contents

Introduction

To be an intimate man could be the challenge of life. To know deeply one's own inner being and to share that knowledge with another person requires the rawest kind of courage. My experience as a therapist has revealed that many men hunger for this perspective on life, and far too many fail to experience a satisfactory exploration of their own inner potential. This is a book for those men, and for the women who share their frustrations.

Deep within each of us is the desire for more knowledge of ourselves and for a vulnerable openness to others in our life space. I hope that this book will contribute to a better understanding and perspective on intimate living. Being a whole man is rewarding and fulfilling. The intent of this book is to facilitate your quest for balance between responsibilities and fulfillment in the relationships of life.

the Intimate man

PART I

Intimacy in the Masculine World

"The man who knows right from wrong and has good judgment and common sense is happier than the man who is immensely rich!

For such wisdom is far more valuable than precious jewels. Nothing else compares with it!"

Proverbs 3:13-15, TLB

CHAPTER ONE

The Fear of Intimacy

"What you have to attempt—to be yourself. What you have to pray for—to become a mirror in which, according to the degree of purity of heart you have attained, the greatness of life will be reflected."

—*Dag Hammarskjold*, Markings

Dan was impressive. He walked into the office with confidence, smiling, appearing to handle easily the tension surrounding meeting another man for the first time. "I really don't have any basic problems," he said: "I think Sharon and I can work this out on our own. In fact, I think we should do that." My reaction to his statement was that perhaps he was right. I've certainly felt that way on many occasions too. I'm a marriage counselor. This scene has occurred thousands of times in my Atlanta office over the last decade. Fifty-seven per cent of my initial appointments for couples are made by men. Dan's wife had come first, but he was here now. About 87 per cent of the husbands whose wives seek help do join them. What draws men to therapy differs little from what draws women—it's called loneliness. We need to be close and yet are afraid to be known. We want independence but fear our isolation from others. Like a two-edged sword intimacy comes, bringing both the fear of and the fascination with closeness into our lives.

In infancy a wonder stirs within us to explore our world internally and externally—to know who and what we are as well as the environment in which we exist. That natural curiosity within is part of the life force; it gives birth to our intellectual, emotional, physical and spiritual search for meaning in the world. The intimate questions of living are Who am I/ Why am I here/ and Where am I going. In the psychological world we call these identity, meaning, and purpose. How we fulfill these demanding quests within us determines the quality of our lives. How comfortable we are with ourselves—our intimate knowledge of our own beings—is at the heart of that quality.

The intimate man will not settle for quantity only in living; he demands an excellence born of security within himself. For him, being alive is more than existing. A full participation in life and an interaction with others is demanded by his sense of honesty. The foundation of intimacy is self-awareness, but that kind of knowledge often grows only from sharing with others.

The intimate man cannot allow himself to wear the mask of a superficial smile, which hides something more of himself, particularly with the significant people in his life. Yet he stumbles at the fear of being known while struggling with the fear of being alone. Because real self-awareness is fulfilled in knowing and being known by others, he needs community to continue his growth. Marriage, family, career, friendships, causes, and faith communities all become parts of this search and fulfill dichotomies within a man.

Dan was superficially impressive. His apparent easy behavior and mannerisms belied his deeper longing. Yet he found difficulty in admitting his need. He had been socialized to expect himself to be independent, capable, and emotionally strong enough not to lean on someone else. He had learned how to close the doors of his life to others, but he had discovered a painful loneliness in being shut up to himself. He was afraid that, if the doors were once opened, he would lose the controls of his life.

As our time together passed, Dan became more comfortable with the idea of being open about himself with me. He shared some confidential things he hadn't told Sharon. I wondered out loud, "Why not?" "I guess she'd be disappointed in me," Dan said quietly. That was the key to his fear—if Sharon knew him like he knew himself, then he assumed she wouldn't like him. He was confessing his own self-displeasure. One of the prison bars for Dan, as for most of us, was self-incriminating feelings. He had failed to live up to some expectations—both those imposed by others and those of his own making. Before that hour was over, Dan had talked about his job frustrations, his feelings about his parents, some of his sexual fears, his need for some male friends, and his dissatisfaction with his faith life.

When we had finished talking, I sensed that Dan was like a lot of other men in the world. Although we hesitate to talk about it openly, we seek to know and be known personally, to love and be loved without conditions, and to discover creatively the fascinating universe in which we exist. The search for this hidden treasure takes us deep within ourselves. The pursuit of this truth will benefit us together, even if we never quite catch it. Let me share with you in this book some of the nuggets from my panning in the stream of human relationships.

CHAPTER TWO

Intimacy Is Not Feminine

"All rising to a great place is by a winding stair."
—Francis Bacon

The most important aspect of the relationship between men and women is not sexuality, it is intimacy. Later, we'll explore in depth this relationship, but first, let's establish a beachhead—*intimacy is not the property of women.*

DIFFERENCES BETWEEN MEN AND WOMEN

In preparing to write this chapter, I searched numerous dictionaries, thesauruses, and word finders. I discovered that the word *femininity* comes from a very physical origin in Latin. *Femina* means "she who suckles." The Greek word for feminine *(thelasa)* comes from a root meaning "nipple." Yet almost all the words in the thesauruses and dictionaries defining or associated with *feminine* involve feelings, tenderness, and a quality of giving—emotional qualities rather than physical characteristics. The words defining *masculine* or *male* tend to involve action, self-reliance, and bravery, etc., rather than physical characteristics.

The dictionaries reflect our unthinking and habitual biases—the way we have been trained to think of men and women. Today we are discovering that we need new definitions of masculine and feminine. Beyond the physical distinctions between men and women, there may be no truly denotative, precise differences. We have inherited connotative, imprecise formulas by which we separate the sexes. Unfortunately, these formulas become "definitions" that easily imprison us, not allowing men and women to be truly themselves because they have to be "a man" or "a woman." Such "definitions" ignore emotion, unless it is expressed with extreme aggressiveness.

In most societies the warring is done by the men and the nesting is done by the women. Most of the distinctions between men and women involve the same kinds of division of responsibility. Neither sex is capable of doing the whole task of living alone, but cooperating means dividing the responsibilities. Functionally, efficiency may result, but at the feeling level those differences blur. The feminist may become militant in her quest for equality, but the man who promotes equality may appear to be weak. We might call him a "masculinist" in contrast to a feminist, but we already have a word which can describe him: *intimate*. Male intimacy arises from three sources: facts, feelings, and force.

Intimacy is based on knowledge. The man who fears intimacy does not want to know himself. Yet that irrationality has been supported by our description of men. Biographies of men are loaded with words such as brave, courageous, self-reliant, intrepid, heroic, upright, etc. These are terms expressive of the spirit of men; but they could well describe women. The pilgrimage to personhood simply has two roads, one called male and the other female. Most of the encounters along those highways are very similar for both sexes.

While we have discouraged women from being aggressive, we have tended to discourage men from self-exploration. Encouragement for factual knowledge and functional capacity surrounds men, but not much concern is expressed for the knowledge of his inner being. He explores outer space to applause from his fellows, but his quest within may be more like exploring a dark cave, alone without a light. Men need to know themselves—physically, intellectually, emotionally, and spiritually. A man who knows himself doesn't confuse that knowledge with what others say about him. He can differentiate between the worlds of reputation and reality. His expectations of himself can be more realistic.

Another step unfolds. Facts alone do not create security in intimacy; feelings are needed. Even though a man may know himself, he may not use that knowledge wisely. The difference between knowledge and wisdom is that which the book of Proverbs states. Good sense constitutes knowledge; wisdom is the discreet and appropriate use of that basic core of facts. And a man's wise use of the facts about himself involves the exploration of his feelings. Too many men have settled for the facts, but have not become wise about themselves by exploring their feelings.

Exploring my feelings means that I need to know not only what I feel, but how I feel, and how to express those feelings. I may know that I need intimacy—that I have the basic hunger—but if I do not express that hunger through my feelings,I cannot satisfy my appetite.

To experience the freedom to feel deeply and to express my feelings means leaving the safety of the predictable and known. I have to discover not only how I can use my strengths but also where I am weak and therefore where I may fail. Such exploration is risky.

You remember our friend Dan. He turned out to have a pretty fair self-knowledge. He had little experience articulating his feelings, but his internal radar picked up clear pictures. What he feared was that Sharon, or someone else, might disapprove of what he saw deep within himself. A part of that perception was based on memories of his grandfather's comments about men. He quoted things he had heard: "A man should make his own mind up—don't take or give advice." Another was "Women depend on men to know; a woman's intuition only means she's got a hunch." And "Make up your own mind, son, and do what you decide; even if you're wrong, don't ever act like it."

Words like these from a man he admired played like tapes in Dan's mind. He was afraid to admit he didn't know or might fail. Often he argued with Sharon or blamed her for a mistake he knew was his own. He began to feel guilt for his dishonesty with himself and his wife. What he learned in the course of exploring himself was that his basic integrity allowed him to be much more comfortable admitting a problem and trying to find a solution; he did not have to try to cover up the original discrepancy. He was becoming secure within himself. Up to then he had been prey to the idea that men have to be right at all times.

ARE MEN ALWAYS RIGHT?

In the early days of television there was an award-winning series called "Father Knows Best." Rerun versions on independent stations are still being shown. Robert Young as the father portrayed calmness and rarely made a mistake. He was always right! If we will look at the character and development of men in our world, we will discover one continuing problem is the "father knows best" syndrome. The patriarchal systems of family life have contributed an expectation that male responsibility is almost infallible.

A couple struggling with the myth that "men are always right" were in my office recently. In this family the wife appeared to be a very supportive, caring person. She talked to her children about her husband's prowess and apparently reinforced their level of appreciation for him. As I worked with them, however, it became apparent that this was her subtle way of avoiding responsibility in the family. By manipulating him into making most decisions, she was able to disavow any basic responsibility for the success or failure of the family

[23]

system. Underneath the "father knows best" ideal was a working style that really meant "mother hides best."

As this couple began to examine their system, this crippling attitude became more apparent to them. They began to develop a new understanding of their interaction. Together we began to work systematically on changing the behavior that supported those expectations. They were eager learners. This basic approach to system change in their relationship allowed more responsibility for her and less "infallibility" for him.

Most marital systems change for only two reasons. One, the pain of continuing the relationship is so great that the couple is willing to do anything to bring about relief. The other, the apparent rewards of a new way of relating, become so inviting that one or both of them are willing to risk moving to that kind of relationship. Those same reasons work for change in any individual's life. Persistent pain or potential pleasures motivate us.

Look at yourself. Are you supporting the "father knows best" system in your relationship with your wife/children? If so, to begin the first step to change that system, look at what you're getting out of the system. What reinforcement, what significant support is your internal man getting from your external behavior?

Tom's agenda was massaging his own ego. He was willing to accept the responsibility of "always being right" in order to build himself up in the eyes of his associates, his family, and his friends. But he began to notice that he was getting into arguments, losing his temper, and finally, failing to function sexually, which he blamed on his wife's inability to excite him. When he finally arrived in my office, most unwillingly, he was close to desperation. But he could not admit his problem! His wife was ready to sue him for a divorce, and many of his business associates and social friends were supporting her in the action. His children were giving him signals that they were uncomfortable with his behavior and putting more distance between themselves and him in their day-to-day relationships.

In the early sessions, he acted rather paranoid about his world. Soon he began to see that his own defensive behavior had contributed to his failing relationships. As he was gently reassured that there were other ways to relate to people, he began to risk the possibility of "failure." He said he wanted "closeness in his relationships." What he saw was distance. He and his wife began to listen to each other. He developed a relationship with other people by stepping off his throne of superiority. He began to risk being "wrong." He allowed people to share in decisions that he made, rather than maintaining constant authoritarian control in every circumstance. He felt his life radically changing. I saw him giving up a phony idea of manhood and accepting a more realistic view of himself.

Being a man is not always being right! *Sometimes being a man means "the ability to acknowledge that I have failed or am wrong about something."* That's a hard lesson for most of us to learn. But acknowledging failure is not a debit on the masculinity scale; it's a credit!

Self-protecting defenses—methods of hiding from people—are the mechanisms that divert our attention from our fears. After awareness of what's happening to us, the second step in the process of growth is acknowledging to someone else what we know about ourselves.

I am more a man when I can face my inadequacies than when I run from them. That's the real promise of intimacy—the development of emotional strength through self-awareness and acknowledgement. The intimate man can become a transparency through which others can discover themselves. Sidney Jourard said that "I only get to know myself when I am willing to reveal who I am to another."[1] The most powerful example of transparent intimacy comes from the New Testament. Jesus Christ reveals himself to us in order that we might truly understand not only who God is but who we are. Personhood takes on its deepest meaning when we hear him saying I AM THAT I AM. This intimacy was expressed by the One who chose to refer to himself often as the "son of man." His idea of intimacy was not feminine; nor must mine be.

CHAPTER THREE

The Intimate Man

"Life is like an onion: you peel one layer at a time, and sometimes you weep."
—Carl Sandburg

The power of intimacy is in its possession. For the individual, the implication cannot be missed. I can never be intimate with another until I know myself. To become familiar with myself lays the foundation for my being close to another person.

INTIMACY AND SELF-ACCEPTANCE

A synonym for intimacy in numerous dictionaries is *familiarity*. For me that not only implies a close knowledge of myself, but involves a feeling of being. However, for my personal sense of intimacy to be more than a breeding ground of contempt, I need the experience of self-acceptance.

I'll use Allan to illustrate this crucial passage into healthy intimacy. Allan and Edith had been married twenty years. He was a handsome man, well-respected in the community, and had been elected to public office on numerous occasions. Edith was petite and charming, but obviously under some stress. The story unfolded over several sessions like this. Dominated by his rather dependent mother, Allan had regularly chosen her wishes over Edith's plans. The rift between them grew. Edith felt rejected, and in a vulnerable moment found solace in the arms of a friend with whom she worked. On an occasion when Allan was to be away from home, Edith invited her friend over to their apartment and eventually they wound up in bed. Allan had a change in plans and returned to find his wife in bed with another man. Obviously enraged, he chased the man out of the apartment and cursed his wife.

After the initial shock wore off, the two of them confessed their sense of failure and Allen even admitted that he himself had been unfaithful. They committed themselves—as the majority of couples I have seen when confronted with marital infidelity do—to another attempt at making their marriage work. Allan still harbored the pain and bitterness in his soul. He was cold and judgmental. That lasted eighteen years until a similar incident brought them to marital therapy.

What Allan discovered when he and Edith committed themselves to work at their marriage was another paradoxical problem. As the oldest child, he had worked diligently to try to please his mother; but imbedded deep within himself was a feeling that he never had. He lived with that frustrated spirit until he married. His mother liked his wife and they got along beautifully. Shortly he began to feel displaced in his mother's life, and subtly began criticizing his wife to both his mother and to her parents who, as he described it, "thought she hung the moon." He wanted closeness with Edith but was jealous of her apparent acceptance by his mother. This envy led to a bitterness that grew like a cancer within him. While Edith felt she accepted, even applauded his achievements, he complained that she was never really pleased. He was reshaping his wife into the image of his mother without recognizing it. He began to use women as pawns in his political and personal life. The blow that got his attention came the day he found his wife with another man.

What Allan learned was that his own refusal to accept the conflict within him became a driving force away from self-knowledge. He could not dare to understand himself; his pain within was too great. Therefore he could not accept himself. He projected his feelings onto others, making them the blame for his problems. He began a tireless campaign for the social underdogs and was a very successful political figure. He just didn't know himself. In an early session he said, "All I want in life is to help people. I want to relieve some of the misery in the city." While that was programmatically true in his official capacity, in his deeply personal world he saw himself as the tired, weary struggler with life, always losing and feeling depressed.

Allan is still working to understand and accept himself. The process he went through illustrates how intimate knowledge of one's self becomes the power to change life. It is accessible to any person willing to explore his own feelings.

FIVE STEPS TO PERSONAL INTIMACY

The following five principles, or steps to intimacy, I describe as the "victory of self-possession over personal emptiness." Step one is to VISUALIZE.

Allan had to see himself and what was happening to him before he could make changes in his behavior. Insight is the ability to focus on and absorb ideas and reflections about ourselves that come to us through the mirrors of life. These mirrors may be formal input—educational experiences, reading books, watching educational television, and other avenues of learning. Or they may take the form of other people and their behavioral reflections from which we learn. This reflective process is one of the key elements in the psychotherapy process.

As Allan visualized himself, he transcended the limits of spontaneous reaction and then was faced with the moment of choice in his behavior. He could see in his own mind the situation with his mother and wife, which had triggered his flight from confrontation. One day he came to see me and was exuberant over his insight: "I discovered something just last night," he said. "I was preparing to give a speech. I asked Edith how she liked the suit I was wearing. When she responded, 'It's fine,' I immediately felt angry, but I didn't know why until I recalled that when my mother said, 'That's fine,' I had always felt furious when she put me down like that. Later when Edith said what a *fine* speech I had given, it all came to me like someone had turned on a light bulb in my head."

Whether Allan's perceptions about his mother were accurate or not is relatively unimportant. What mattered was that he understood his anger and was able to visualize his poor reaction. On reflection he envisioned a more appropriate behavior and responded positively. He was no longer a prisoner to unexamined reactions within him.

The second step is the one Allan took in our visit: VERBALIZE. Many men are like computers; they store information about feelings, but it is rarely utilized. In order for change to begin, a man needs to find words to express his inner feelings. Sometimes it is a struggle; feelings of vulnerability or potential failure have to be overcome.

What begins deep within me may be a disorganized impulse, but my attempts to articulate shape the energy into words to which others can respond. Verbalizing is extremely important. It is a process that protects me from two errors: my own assumptions and yours. When I fear that something I say will sound stupid or even boastful, I remain inexpressive. My assumptions are untried. No one else can challenge the judgment I have made about myself. If I don't share with you, you are only left with your assumptions about what I'm thinking or feeling. In either case, the only way of contact is through the process of verbalizing my thoughts or feelings.

Edith's complaints were varied, but what she most frequently said was, "How can I know what he's thinking if he doesn't talk to me?" Inexpressive males are often struggling within themselves for words that describe their feelings, thoughts, or reactions; frequently they lose the battle and remain silent. Sometimes the woman relating to an inexpressive male has to develop patience in order not to put her words in his mouth.

The third step is to VITALIZE your insight. More is required for change in behavior than words; the insight must be given form and action. Vitalizing means giving "life-action" to a perception of one's self or another. Allan had to begin to act differently before Edith could see that he was serious about what he had said to her. An inner decision to do something brings relief within me. Putting that decision into action builds my confidence and enhances future possibilities of change.

The fourth step is VALIDATE your progress. Growth can be seen only over an extended period of time. The time frame allows me to assess my steps from the point of beginning to the point of evaluation. When I verify or assess my actions, there is the assurance of progress or focus on the point of failure. Allan was able to validate his progress, not only by the presence of positive feelings about himself, but also through the responses Edith began to make. One day she said, "I really have a hard time having confidence that Allan's behavior will be maintained, but I can't deny that he really is functioning differently these days. He's now that husband I've been asking him to be."

The final step is VOW to continue with the positive areas of change you discover through your validation. Allan's commitment for change in his life was a deeply personal experience. He described it by saying: "I hope Edith will like the changes I'm making. I think she will, but I feel so keenly about these insights that I must change for my own sake." That's the key to the process: wanting to know myself for the benefit it brings me as a person. Self-intimacy protects me from self-deception and builds my sense of self-appreciation. This is the foundation for all other experiences of intimacy.

In summary the process is: visualize, verbalize, vitalize, validate, and vow. These simple steps can help you to become a man who is intimate with himself.

CHAPTER FOUR

The Intimate Father

"God's most insistent call to us will always seem a sort of silence, since His language isn't what we expect."

—Louis Evely

A question quite frequently asked by mothers concerns the emotional development of their children. Unfortunately, too few fathers ask those types of questions. Bill was an exception. He asked, "How can I help my son develop this thing called intimacy?" In trying to help him find an answer for his question I developed these guidelines for teaching your son intimacy. Try them on for size in your experience.

First, *be open with your son.* You can't teach him anything you don't really model. If you can risk sharing your feelings with him, then he gets the idea that openness is the appropriate behavior. If you are not open with him, no matter what you may say, he will not learn intimacy. He learns from your behavior rather than your words. Intimacy is a learned experience. Your son trusts his feelings through watching you trust your own. His comfort about sharing himself increases as he experiences your comfort in opening yourself to him.

The second most significant model is *the relationship to your wife*. Charlie Shedd says that "the best Dad is a good lover." On a plaque in my office are these words "the best gift that a father can give his children is to love their mother." As your son sees the reality of your relationship, he comes to appreciate what intimacy with a woman is. What he observes supports his instincts toward similar behavior on his part in the future. He will be able to sense the atmosphere in the home as well as to see your cheerfulness in sharing tasks and resolving the differences the two of you encounter in living.

The touchiest years for teaching your son intimacy occur when he becomes a teen-ager. He may withdraw and become moody. He may become so involved in his peer world that he has little time for you. *Keep reaching out to him*, even when he may reject you. These lessons in modeling may be the most effective ones you ever show him. You can teach him how to react to disappointment, how to handle rejection, how to listen non-judgmentally, and how to support another person while that person makes a decision without your son reaching it for him. These may be critical examples for him later in his experience as a father.

The fourth guideline calls for you to *put your values on the line* as he formulates his own principles for living. Probably most fathers would wish for their sons to adopt the basic rules by which they themselves live, but that cannot be accomplished merely by telling your son what those principles are. He will test them against all the other ideas he receives. He will probably question you and your ideas. He may even appear to reject most of your values. Your intimate strength may be displayed at these points more than ever in your lives together. Let him experience your strength as caring and your tenderness as strength. That's intimacy in action. Paradoxically, intimacy is the strength to be vulnerable. That vulnerability deeply supports your strength. Fathers enhance respect from their sons more in moments of loving confrontation than in times of detailed instruction.

Communication is the doorway to intimacy. Keeping the lines open constitutes the foundation of the relationship. Talking, touching, and writing are important direct ways to share one's self. Sharing tasks, experiencing recreation, and being together in community and worship activities communicates who you are as well. I have found that writing becomes a vehicle for special communication with my children over the years.

Here is one of the attempts to share these ideas with my youngest son, on his eighteenth birthday!

Dear Jeff,

Happy Birthday, Son! Eighteen years between us have slipped by so quickly. Soon you'll be leaving for college; and while you'll always have a home base with us, your own sense of personhood calls you into a time of transition where home will be the place you are and not where we live.

I was proud of you as a baby. That perpetual smile on your face attracted almost everyone to you, young and old. You seemed to develop friendships so easily, and I especially admired the way you adjusted to several of the moves we made when you were quite young. You've always been a competitor. Perhaps being the third child teaches you to hold your own before someone else gets what you want. The only danger I see is that your fierce spirit of independence could isolate you at times from the opportunity to let others share with you. I respect your right to make personal choices. I've tried to do that since you were very young, but I want you to see that respect as support not disregard.

Since today is your birthday, I want to share with you my hopes for the next eighteen years. I really think it takes that long for parents to judge how well they've done at helping their children mature. I wish for you a continuing growth in your virile physique and all the pleasures of knowing that you are a handsome man. Enjoy other people's admiring glances, but not too much. Don't let yourself be satisfied with external appearances and miss developing the inner strength that shows through to make a man genuinely attractive.

I want for you the joy of feeling close to other people. Grow to be an intimate man—one who knows himself well and is willing to take the time to understand others. Growth like that arises from deliberate choices. You'll be tempted to learn only how to manipulate people to get what you want but not to let them know you. Not everyone will want to know you, and you'll need to choose selectively the people you share with, but don't miss the most satisfying levels of living by being remote. Intimacy is where life is—physically, emotionally, and spiritually.

Physical curiosity looms as the strongest drive toward intimacy for you now. Sexual relationships can be one of the most rewarding pleasures in life or they can reinforce your sense of isolation. The loneliest people I know are those who are physically intimate but remain closed to other levels of relationships. You only have one body; be careful how and with whom you share it. Invest your physical and emotional resources wisely.

Finally, Jeff, I pray for the greatest satisfaction that life can hold for you, to be close to God. I love you—probably more than you know; and because I do, I've tried to be there when

[37]

you really needed me during these first eighteen years. Your eternal Father can and will *always* be with you. Stay close to him as you mature. Proverbs says, "Only good men enjoy life to the full," and I believe that. I pray that you will be a good man who gets all that God has for you in life.

Love,

Dad

Intimacy involves an ever-unfolding pattern of growth and risk within one's self and toward others. Like any muscle, the more it is used the stronger and more effective it becomes; so the intimate man continues to plumb his own depths and share his discoveries with others, as they share theirs with him. Like wisdom, intimacy is a process. The words of Solomon summarize it well: "Wisdom is a tree of life . . . happy is the man who keeps on eating it" (Proverbs 3:18 *TLB*).

CHAPTER FIVE

The Development of Intimacy

Intimacy defined apart from God has too small a context for me. I find more meaning in every level of intimate contact in relation to his larger universe. I find no conflict between theology and psychology, although there are numerous contrasts between the psychologists and the theologians. The truth is the crucial or dividing line. Higher than any other form of truth is personhood, and the ultimate in theological doctrine is the personhood of God, especially as revealed in the incarnation of Christ on earth. God's own desire for intimacy with man becomes the backdrop of all relationships.

Understanding God as Father is a starting point. Textbooks about psychological development say it is difficult for a person to appreciate what the role of a good father is if he has had no model. Of course, if he had a "bad" father, then it would be very difficult for him to think of God as a "good" Father. The theological world is full of references to God as *Father*. I sat down the other day and tried to say what having God as a Father means to me.

[39]

CLOSENESS

One of the first things I discovered is that having God as my father means *closeness*. As a boy when I had a paper route, my dad would get up early on rainy Sunday mornings to go with me in the car and help me deliver the unusually large papers that we had on Sundays. I always appreciated that, and I felt close to my dad at those times we were working together. I remember feeling close when we went hunting together or did some of the other father-son activities, although these were somewhat infrequent.

As I think about God, the overriding quality I want to maintain in my relationship to him is this quality of closeness. Fatherhood is a kind of automatic door to intimacy. There are some things a father has access to in the lives of his children that no one else has. In the same way there are some things that a child has access to in the life of his father that no one else does. God's fatherhood only becomes a reality when we allow him to be close to us and to share our lives.

INTEGRITY

A second important term describing man's relationship to God is *integrity*. For me the hierarchy of personal integrity is summed up in three questions:

Is what I'm about to do in keeping with my character and personhood?

Is what I'm about to do in keeping with

[40]

commitments that I have made to the intimate members of my world (my wife, my family, etc.)?

Is what I'm about to do going to serve as an example to anyone else who may view that action?

God as Father provides me with a base of integrity. God made me to be a man with certain potential, ability, and capacity that I want to fulfill. Sin is not so much an act against God, but a failure to live out God's gifts in one's experience. My "sin" against my father would be to fail to respond to the things he has given me as his child. So in my relationship to God, sin is failing to live out my potential as a person. For me that potential entails far more freedom than limitation. God's fatherhood is not a set of rules against which I measure the acceptability of my life before him, but is instead an encouragement to be all that I can be as his son.

PRESENCE

A third thing that God's fatherhood means to me is in the area of loneliness. Because I believe that not only is there an existent God, but a personal being whom I call Father, I can never be alone in the universe.

I remember reading for the first time those words from Robert Frost's poem about home: "Home is the place where, when you have to go there, they have to take you in." As long as a person has a home (or family) he always has a place to go when he needs it. As long as a man has a Father, there is someone he can turn to. As long as God exists, I as a man do not have to be lonely. I am persuaded that being a child of God is not the result of being bribed by a sense of needing God's approval or by the promise of material goods if I act the way I ought to so I'll receive God's blessings. It is not the result of being threatened with the punishment of hell or some other inscrutable judgment. It is instead the result of a kind of persuasion that grows out of my loneliness.

I am aware that there are two kinds of fears that drive a man. The first is the fear that "someone will know him as he really is." Because of this fear he wears a "mask" to keep other people away from him. He hides and pretends and deceives. But there is a far greater fear in all of us—the fear that "no one will ever know us." If no one ever knows me, my loneliness remains intact and is the most powerful force in my experience. So one of the goals in life is to let someone enter into the secret world within us and know us as we are. The "new birth" that is spoken of in the New Testament is the moment when I allow God to permeate the innermost part of my being. At that moment I open myself up to the loss of loneliness and the experience of having a friend who is my Father.

DISCOVERING WHOLENESS

Outside my own family I derive personal satisfaction from my work. I feel very fortunate to be able to enter many people's lives. One of the ways this occurs is in my personal growth groups.

These experiences are limited to eight adult men and women who meet together for twenty-five hours over a ten-week period. One of the major aspects of this experience is the opportunity to disclose oneself to others and in the process come to know oneself better.

There is a constant reaffirmation in this process as I see men and women feeling more confident about themselves as they learn to relate to each other honestly. This has become a "religious" experience for many group members. They have not only become aware of their own feelings and the feelings of others, but have become aware of the presence of God in the group.

While there is no specific theological instruction in these groups, it has never surprised me that people experience God here. Where wholeness occurs, God is present, even if not acknowledged. For me, that provides significant data about God as Father.

As I invest myself in another person by disclosing who I am, a new dimension of my value and worth is inherently given to him. As he reveals himself to me, he decreases my loneliness by bridging the distance between us.

I read a clear account in biblical history of God's sharing himself with me. As I have responded, I have discovered who my Father really is. That discovery has freed me to find hope in all the dimensions of my relationships to other men and women—hope about being a man in today's world.

I am not everything I have described in this book at all times, but I have experienced the reality of every idea here. I know of no greater hope than to be more of a man today than I was yesterday and less than I will be tomorrow. As Robert Browning said, "A man's reach should exceed his grasp."

Self-acceptance is based then on being a part of God's creation, which he described as "good." That is not self-righteousness. True religion means "living to show that God is your personal Father," and your life is the measure of his parenting. Jesus said, "Let your light so shine before men, that they may see your good works and give glory to your father who is in heaven" (Matt. 5:16 RSV).

The most demanding part of our faith is in its application to relationships. Part two leads us to explore the intimate man's relationship to women.

PART II

Masculinity in the Feminine World

"It is possible to give away and become richer! It is also possible to hold on too tightly and lose everything."

Proverbs 11:24 (TLB)

CHAPTER SIX

The Earliest Intimacy

"You came into my life and loved me and somehow I became me."

—Chantal

The earliest intimacy of our lives is the physical relationship to the woman we call mother. She has the first input and claim on the potential of our emotional development. Being a mother may not supersede being a father, but none of us knows the other side of that experience. What we know is interaction with the women in our world. In those early years it is predominantly a woman's world to which we are introduced. Think of all the things that women—nurses, mothers, grandmothers, big sisters, "Aunt Sarahs"—do to and for babies! It is surprising how little practical help has been given to men on how they grow up or how to survive in a world predominantly populated by females. Sigmund Freud suggests that in the first two years of life a child considers himself a majestic infant. He doesn't distinguish between his wishes and those of other people in his world. He demands what satisfies his own needs. He cries and others are to respond. Initially he finds satisfaction through the oral cavity. He brings things into his world via his mouth—occasionally he discovers that some things don't belong there! As he grows he learns eventually to see himself as a part instead of the total universe.

During the second or anal phase he learns that he can give or withhold what others want from him. Failure to adjust in this period of life hampers his later growth process. Successful development at this level provides a foundation for learning self-discipline and respect for others. On secure sharing experiences he builds positive relationships for handling the conflicts of his future. Unresolved struggles for personal power affect his concern and sensitivity to others' needs throughout his life. Passive control as a way of relating can often be traced to this time when a man begins his struggle for autonomy.

The discovery of his sexuality marks a new period in his development. He is different from his mother. His curiosity about the distinctions between male and female has begun. How he handles this knowledge and his subsequent comfort with the new facts he gains influence how he survives in this world. He is becoming a man.

BECOMING A MAN

Being physically born a male only begins the process of becoming a man. Significant influences contribute positively or negatively to your sense of masculinity. Almost every man I have seen in my office can identify a single person who helped shape his early life. Surprisingly it may not always be a parent. Someone else may see you as "a special little man" and invest time and energy in your development.

My grandmother was notorious in the larger family unit because of her favoritism toward me. I don't know how I developed "the special grandchild" label, but I now look back with a sense of appreciation. Her attention to little things that others overlooked reinforced my growing self-esteem. Her constant reassurance helped build a base of confidence within me. She laughed with me—and at me—which helped me develop a sense of humor. She wasn't psychologically astute; she just knew how to love a little boy. Every young man needs someone like that in his early life. Without it he misses a unique contribution to his own exploration of loving relationships later.

The seeds for the field of intimacy are planted during these first years of a man's experience. Later, we'll explore their development more thoroughly. The seminal moment occurs when any significant person impresses you with the fact that he is aware of your uniqueness. You become psychologically inducted into personhood through such encounters.

BEING A MAN

Boys are special to their fathers, brothers, grandfathers, and uncles. They discover models in these men. Older men are guides in the process of self-identification for boys who emulate them. Men bear great responsibilities in teaching, deliberately or unknowingly, what it means to be "manly." *All* men teach *some* boys lessons that affect their future. The attitudes shown and the actions displayed powerfully demonstrate the *masculine* patterns. Most important among these is the way men show boys how to relate to women.

Ben paused a moment and read the words on the poster on my office wall: "The greatest gift a father can give his children is to love their mother." He seemed a little sad when he reflected: "I've had a hard time learning to say 'I love you' to my wife, as you know. I'm just now getting in touch with the fact that when my dad died—I was only three—I only heard Mother say those words until I became a teenager. I guess I've thought women spoke and men listened, but I'm beginning to enjoy telling Marge and the children how I feel." Ben was twenty-eight years old and just beginning to explore the fun of verbal intimacy. He was a bright young man—intelligent, articulate, and handsome. He had simply missed out on a male role model who verbalized feelings.

A MOTHER'S IMPRINT

Without a doubt mothers are dominant in the sense of intimacy a man develops. In our society no other relationship is as potent as that of mother to son. Someone other than the physical mother may fill this vital spot in your life because of absence, abdication, or abuse; but no one has such natural access to your emotions as does your mother. Her invisible, psychological umbilical cord can strangle you in adult years. Her remembered nurture can sustain you long after her body is in the grave.

Mothers begin our adventure in the world of women, but there are more females in our futures. Sisters, grandmothers, aunts, teachers, etc. play their own special roles. Their contributions play a part in our understanding of ourselves, especially in the arena of intimacy.

I've come to the conclusion that chauvinism is produced in males by the females in their lives, especially their mothers. Your mother had the first opportunity to demonstrate to you what women feel about men. She told you how she felt about your father and the other men in your life. From that you got your first insight in the strength of a woman or the reactions she may have to a man.

Women who are dependent teach their sons that other women will lean on them. Women who dominate or abuse teach their sons not to trust women. The lessons also apply to fathers and daughters. Ask now what your mother taught you, not for the purpose of blaming, but to learn about yourself. Not all of your knowledge about women or about intimacy came from your mother, but hers was the earliest input.

How you have built on her input by adherence to what she taught or by reaction will determine a lot about your feelings and your experiences of intimacy with women. Fortunately, you are not responsible for the people that happen in your life, but you are responsible for the way you react to them.

As you read these chapters, some ideas about how you have reacted may fall into place. You may find yourself thinking back to your childhood and teen-age years. You may well locate a significant person who has had a determined influence on your experience of intimacy. When you come to this insight, you can begin to change—positively, some of your behavior in intimate situations.

How you have grown up may determine where you are emotionally at this point in life, but you have the potential to learn about yourself and to change in ways that please you. This knowledge is the beginning of self-intimacy.

CHAPTER SEVEN

Grow Up, Little Man!

"Love does not dominate; it cultivates."
—Goethe

Few of us can remember what it's like to be a baby. A baby boy gets treated in pretty much the same way as a baby girl. He is cuddled, smiled at by all sorts of adults who want to see if he can smile, has teeth, or will cry! He hears the same "noises" and sees the same faces made at him as she does. As long as he's a baby that's fine, but there comes a point in a boy's life when things change. (I am aware of present research that indicates these differences in treatment may begin from the earliest moments of life. The changes, however, are unquestionably clear in the period from twenty-four to forty-eight months.) It's no longer acceptable to be a "little boy"—now he's got to be a "little man." This is a perceptibly harsh change for many developing male egos. Why shouldn't he be able to go on crying when something hurts, or playing with the dolls, or enjoying soft textures, or occasionally wanting to be the mother when he plays "house" in the family or with the neighborhood children? Why should he now always have to be strong? Maybe no one knows why, but it becomes a problem many men struggle with for a lifetime.

CONTROLLING EMOTIONS

One of the common complaints that family counselors hear is that husbands are unemotional, preoccupied, absorbed in what's going on in their minds or with the pressures of their world. Let's take a look at Joe (and you know that isn't his real name), an engineer. He deals in a world that's precise, a world in which he can always find the "right" answer. No matter what the situation is, he keeps struggling or going back to the drawing board and to the formulas until he discovers the appropriate response. He may have chosen to be an engineer simply because he was trained all of his life to control his emotions; to make things come out in precision steps with no unexplained part or loose ends left over is his task.

FUNCTIONAL VERSUS INTIMATE

Rules work well for Joe in his professional career; but when he begins relating to a woman on a one-to-one, intimate basis, he finds himself with no rules, few guidelines, and many frustrations! Inside, he may be asking where all the freedom has gone. Does his life consist of nothing but responsibilities now? He married Mary because she respected him and made him feel important. He enjoyed the feeling of "having all the answers," but her dependence on him for constant stroking and reassurance of his love grows very old for Joe at times. He wants her to learn her own role and function smoothly without expecting and demanding constant emotional reassurance from him.

Mary, on the other hand, feels disappointed that Joe is withdrawn and distant. She no longer feels able to relate to him. Failing to develop emotional closeness in their marriage, they came for counseling.

"Why are you two here?" I asked. Mary blurted out her story in almost hysterical tones while Joe sat stone-faced and silent. "I'm here because she's driving me crazy with those emotional outbursts! Can you help her?" Before Mary could retort I interceded to describe a diagnostic plan that Joe could "buy."

She had a problem—he was it! The expectations he had attempted to fulfill as he grew up left him few options in manhood. He certainly wasn't what Mary expected in a husband.

COWBOY OR PLAYBOY?

Jack Balswick, a noted sociologist at the University of Georgia, said that *men fall basically into two categories: the cowboy and the playboy (Why I Can't Say I Love You,* Waco, Tex: Word Books, 1978). The cowboy is a rather bashful, John Wayne, western-type man who is more at home with his horse than he is with his lady friend. When she seductively bats her eyes at him all he can reply is, "Aw, shucks, ma'am!" He is more at ease stroking and nuzzling his horse than he is kissing and fondling a woman. He is a man of action and function. Give him room to roam without too many restrictions.

The playboy on the other hand is suave, debonair, and casual in his attitude toward woman. He is rarely satisfied with *one* woman and constantly in search of something more—that elusive woman who will fulfill his fantasy! He places little value on any woman in particular and is unable to make a genuine commitment to one. He notices every woman, is intrigued by her uniqueness, and in his own way he needs to find a special place in the life of every woman he knows.

The woman married to the cowboy may console herself in the fact that he doesn't say much; by the way he acts and the kind of commitment he shows to her, he demonstrates that he does love her. But the woman married to the playboy soon begins to feel used and "passed by" in the parade of younger, more exciting and more stimulating women.

Joe, the engineer, would have to be called a cowboy rather than a playboy. He depended on his actions rather than his words. He wanted logic not emotion in life and in his wife. Somewhere in the formation of his ideals for manhood a strong implant said, "men think and act—women feel." Unfortunately, Mary's expectation called for a sensitive, compassionate man—much like her own father was. Their counseling process involved helping them to understand the differences in their own expectations. Then they began to build new goals for their relationship.

If you find yourself uneasy, shy and reserved, you will probably develop a cowboy stance in life. You may engage in heroic feats and enjoy your "silent strength." However, your loneliness in relationships will remain. Very often your "bashfulness" can be a manipulative way of getting attention from women. You may have mastered, knowingly or unwittingly, the art of using your silence to engage the admiration of women. The maternal juices of many women flow strongly toward the shy and introverted men. The quiet man is a mystery to be solved.

The "playboy" type excites a woman's passions. Because he focuses on her, momentarily she feels as though she is the *only* woman in the world. So, the Don Juan is afforded a key to her soul and sometimes to her body. His promise of love completely disarms her—or so it seems. Yet a temporary quality in his devotion undermines the playboy's relationship to her. He can in no way fulfill all his promises, so he fulfills none of them, and therefore remains lonely.

TAKING THE INITIATIVE

Every male in the world has to face the expectations with which he has grown up and decide how he's going to respond to them. Both husbands and wives resist fulfilling each other's expectations, and this results in constant arguments. Many men make the tragic, sometimes fatal, marital mistake of saying, "I will not meet your expectations." Then they fail to live out their own potential as individuals. In working with numbers of men I have seen the man with great locked-up potential who refuses to be the kind of husband his wife wants him to be; and in so doing he often fails to *be a father* to his children! Or in the process of refusing to be the kind of husband she expects him to be, he fails to be a husband at all.

Men make choices about the way they fulfill the expectations of the women in their lives. An irresponsible man cops out by refusing to meet her expectations and offering nothing in return. In the maturing process a man distinguishes between another person's expectation and his own. In that transition he discovers the goals that will guide him to maturity as a man.

A positive thing about the broad socialization process of most boys is that it usually leaves them some kind of initiative. For all the double standards we hold about sexuality—at least we held them until the Women's Lib Movement hit us—the man was given the opportunity to take the initiative and the woman was left with the responsibility of maintaining it. In the past, society tolerated boys doing some "ridiculous" things in their maturing process because "boys will be boys," and every man has in him some "wild oats" that he must sow! In this part of the socialization process is the key that every man can use to unlock the doors of his own potential. Examine the expectations of others; and look at your own qualifications and resources! Begin to develop the unique man that you really are. Part of who you are will be indicated by the woman with whom you chose to share your life.

No matter how mature a man becomes, his desire to relate to a woman in a significant way will play a vital role in his life. Curiosity craves fulfillment not only in his loins and his head but in his heart.

CHAPTER EIGHT

Unchained Curiosity

"People are lonely because they build walls instead of
bridges."

—Poster, Abbey Press

THE CHILD WITHIN

The dullest men I know are those who have never
allowed the child in them to develop. They are also
the most vulnerable men in relationships to
women. As the transactionalist analysts point out,
we have within us various parts, or ego states,
which can be identified by the way we function. The
parent part is both critical and nurturing while the
child state is curious, submissive, and rebellious.
The *adult* has the responsibility of managing the
conflict between these two functions.

How quickly a man passes from being a child to
being an adult. "When I Was One-and-Twenty," by
A. E. Housman, catches this poignant transition.

When I was one-and-twenty
I heard a wise man say,

"Give crowns and pounds and guineas
  But not your heart away;
Give pearls away and rubies
  But keep your fancy free."
But I was one-and-twenty,
  No use to talk to me.

When I was one-and-twenty
  I heard him say again,
"The heart out of the bosom
  Was never given in vain;
'Tis paid with sighs a plenty
  And sold for endless rue."
And I am two-and-twenty
  And oh, 'tis true, 'tis true.

Often as adults we are no longer able to be free, spontaneous, and curious about our worlds. We appear to be trapped in our responsibilities and commitments.

Sometimes in group therapy, when fantasy experiences are provided, the "little boy" in men emerges again. I'll never forget Bill. He was an executive, handsome, suave, and extremely controlled. He said the right words, did the proper things, and acted in the appropriate manner in almost every situation. But one night he allowed the child in him to fantasize about some experiences in his early years on the farm. It was a transformation. His face loosened, his eyes brightened, and his body relaxed. More important was that he became interested in other people in the group. He became curious about others. He listened, he asked questions, and he thought about the answers he received. He became once more a little boy.

That childlike curiosity is part of what keeps a man alive. It is also part of his anxiety too. Sören Kierkegaard called this anxiety "the alarming possibility of being able." Part of man's fear and part of his ability to dream are caught in this curious, childlike interest in himself and others.

TRUE MATURITY

The greatest gift an adult woman has given to me as an adult man is the rediscovery of my "inner child." My wife is the "eternal child," ever fascinated with little accomplishments and always thrilled by the smallest of gifts. Since I am somewhat compulsive, we face a number of conflicts. However, her patience and exuberance with life were too contagious! After twenty-six years I've decided it's more fun to *cultivate* the inner child than to *crucify* it. I remember early struggles in our marriage that resulted in great part from the dominance of the "parent" in me. My life seemed to skip from age six to age twenty-six, leaving no time for being a teen-ager—that transition period in which childishness finds its blend with maturity.

As I struggled with my own identity in psychotherapy, I discovered a helpful book, *Your Inner Child of the Past,* by W. Hugh Missildine (Simon & Schuster, 1963). My own curiosity to know more about the "child" in me has contributed to the maturing process in my life. For many, like me, there is a rapid transition from childhood to manhood. The consequence is the death, or at least a severe restricting, of the inner child. No longer can he be free to "play"; he is a man. He may even admonish himself with the words of Paul, "When I was a child, I spoke like a child, I thought like a child, I reasoned like a child; when I became a man, I gave up childish ways" (I Cor. 13:11 RSV). This man, who takes his faith seriously, finds that there is a double bind: the assumed expectations of male maturity and his quest for spiritual growth. Disregarding the biblical promise and thrust about joy, this Christian can get *deadly* serious about "maturity."

What is maturity? It is a willingness to assume responsibility for one's own thoughts, feelings, words, and actions. Nothing in that definition forbids joy in one's accomplishments or laughter at one's faults. In many ways the phrase "unchained curiosity" best expresses man's continuing growth physically, emotionally, and spiritually.

As he extends his muscles and physical limits, a man's body grows. In the quest for spiritual maturity, his soul grows. Interestingly, Jesus said only those who could become "as a little child" could enter the kingdom of heaven. Development beyond "the new birth" is seen as "growing up into Christ."

Physical growth seems to happen naturally and without much demand in most of us. The athlete, however, can experience significant changes by a deliberate program of training. He may not only add pounds but strength to his body's capacity. In the same way, the undeveloped mind and spirit can be expanded through reading, meditation, reflection, and interchange with others. The need for intimate sharing in this process becomes apparent. Whether I share with a mentor or a fellow struggler, I need support in my mental and spiritual growth efforts. My willingness to share with others helps me cope with my loneliness as well as satisfy my curiosity.

Every man has unanswered queries in his mind and heart. Those empty spots in his life are the results of unfulfilled wishes, unsatisfied needs, unaffirmed instincts, unrealized potentials, and uncertain directions in his person. There is a need to "ask" in every man. He asks for information, for responses, and for wishes fulfilled. Most of all, he asks for affirmation of who he is. When he hobbles the colt of curiosity, he will find that the pasture is too limited to raise a thoroughbred—the mature and fully developed animal. He will remain in some respects undeveloped, immature. The man who no longer allows his queries to be expressed begins to accept the limits that ultimately result in death—the final break in his physical relationships.

CURIOSITY—BONDAGE OR FREEDOM?

Bob is a young man with much potential and a great curiosity about how he relates to his world. He sees himself as being aggressive and industrious in his working style, but he actually relates to people in a very passive and placating manner. He needs external assurance that he has the approval and affirmation of another person before he is willing to make a decision. This puts a great deal of pressure on his wife. She is called upon to make most of the affirmations and reassurances that are necessary in his experience with the world.

But her support isn't always enough. In his immaturity and need for reassurance Bob allows his natural curiosity to develop into an insatiable desire for affirmation from new relationships. Because of this need he has an unsatisfactory vocational record, with numerous job changes. But he also allows it to feed his quest for female affirmation and impel him into another affair with another woman. When I first saw Bob in counseling, he was unwilling to accept the child within him and therefore was prisoner to its power. Once he began to realize that it was acceptable for him to have feelings that he considered to be childish or immature, he began to grapple with that part of himself and to make progress in his life-style.

So many of us are afraid to accept any part of ourselves we cannot control, but contained with that refusal lies the loss of our freedom. *Freedom is the willingness to live even when I am not in control of the circumstances or situations of my life.* That sense of liberty makes it possible to face things within myself that I do not like. When I am willing to acknowledge my uncertainty or insecurity, then I am more likely to avoid those feelings or situations where I'm not in control. Acknowledging the inner child, therefore, sustains my possibilities for growth by giving me the freedom to enter new or difficult situations. The curiosity within leads me to discoveries of significance along the paths of life. It is the force which pulls me forward to new opportunities. People rarely discover anything while backing up. The freedom to risk forging ahead brings a special reward. It works in relationships too.

When we fear others, we "wall them out." When we reach for others, we "bridge" to them. Men and women make those choices toward each other. Introversion is an escape from others. In relationships, however, to escape within is to insulate our loneliness and increase our depression.

DUETS OF DISCOVERY

In college I had a roommate who was a loner. He was a brilliant student and very congenial as a living partner. He was afraid of people, especially females, until he met the girl who became his wife. Their romance, unseen by many because of their subtle exchanges, was like the blooming of a flower in the desert. Two quiet people, each secretly curious about the other, began to open themselves. They spanned a human chasm by their discovery of each other. A more demanding girl would have turned him further inward; a suave and sophisticated boy would have made her feel more inadequate. He found balance in her, and his life was never the same.

They explored together. He learned about a woman as she opened herself to him. My roommate needed time to become a man; he fortunately found a patient partner. Some men are not so fortunate!

CHAPTER NINE

The Intimate World of Men and Women

This is a male treatise for liberation! But let's not fight with women. Let us lay down the encrusted weapons of the role warfare and explore a lively and enlivened encounter, enriched by differences and fused by similarities.

It happens like this:

Scott gently took her hand and spoke the two most important words of human interaction—"forgive me." Out of her hurt, Sue burst into tears; she nestled her head on his shoulder and sobbed. His tears quietly rolled down his cheeks and joined hers on his shirt. A painful confrontation had brought an exhilarating release and a moment of unfettered intimacy.

As I watched Sue and Scott, I wanted to remove my shoes because I had the feeling of standing on holy ground. I had been into the confessional with them, and I rejoiced as they experienced a sense of renewal at the altar of their personal and marital pilgrimage. When I had first met them, I thought that a battlefield was the most appropriate analogy of their relationship. She almost made the concrete floor of the office shake as her one-hundred-ten-pound body pounded down the carpeted hall, and she walked into my office. She sat down as though unburdening her heels of a load. Crossing her legs she showed her fidgety energy level by constantly moving her feet.

Scott seemed withdrawn and angry. His large, athletic frame was tense even though he tried to smile and went through the preliminary introductions with appropriate public relations skills. Although he was only thirty-two, he seemed seriously intent about this visit to a family therapist.

I was soon to learn that Sue had liked their previous therapist but he did not relate to her well in their interviews. Now Sue felt under duress in my office. From that shaky beginning seven sessions earlier, the three of us arrived at the peak of intense intimacy. On the surface it was a dramatic about-face. At the inner level they had taken a series of calculated risks, and they won!

Scott's risks involved admitting his personal guilt, camouflaged by being overly critical of Sue. Behind his smokescreen was an extramarital affair. Sue's risks included acknowledging her continued commitment to Scott and handling her pain of rejection and disappointment.

As they sank into each other's arms on the office couch, I allowed them some solitude without words. While I watched I thought of the similarities between underwater exploration and male-female intimacy.

Men and women spend much more time planning, fantasizing, and scheming about their intimate moments than they do actually experiencing them. Like divers, their exploration must be planned, equipped, and executed very carefully. Changes in the emotional conditions can wreak havoc in a couple's life just as atmospheric disturbances do a diver's most calculated plans.

Yet the successful discovery exhilarates the undersea explorer when it occurs. So does the excitement of touching deeply the secret places of another human life.

Intimacy is where the worlds of men and women converge—physically, psychologically, and spiritually. Ultimately, behind the masks of bravado and mystique the facades of isolation or dependency, the risks of the naked soul lie. When he meets her there, they have come home to each other.

Scott and Sue had arrived at that priceless meeting spot. A session later they were still on a high plane, but both wondered about the ebb and flow of their emotional tide. "How do we stabilize our relationship?" Scott queried.

Perhaps you've wondered that too. Then explore with me some of the male and female inlets of life to discover some of the secrets of stability.

Let's begin with the choice to marry.

CHAPTER TEN

How Do You Know You're Ready?

"At the heart of love, there is a simple secret: the lover lets the beloved be free."

—D. James Kennedy

She complained that he should be ready by now. Her problem was a marriage—more specifically, marriage to a certain man. When I met her man, I understood more of her problem.

"How do I know she's the one I should marry?" he asked. "Bachelorhood has been awfully good to me." His question deserved careful thought from me and deliberation for himself. At thirty, he had been quite independent of women. "I know how to date a girl," and he described the intricate details of an evening he was planning. "Women are a fantastic challenge—until you get them—then they are a burden!"

Bob made me think a lot about why men and women marry. He knew the traditional answers as well as I did. It would please his parents and hers! The Church would bless their union. He could settle down and spend less energy looking for dates.

He had gotten engaged the way many young people do—without *serious* thought, but as the wedding date drew nearer, panic set in! And weddings are enough to frighten most men.

Let's look closely at our marriage rituals. There she is in all her glory, and there he is—nervous! Her "catch" is on display for all the world (gathered for the wedding) to see. Probably nobody feels more like an extra thumb than the groom at a wedding rehearsal or ritual.

In a more serious vein, the divorce rate reflects the invalidity of any of the serious vows we take. Almost half our marriages in the United States end in divorce. Many of those statistics are young people who marry much too soon, or at least before they are ready to make that decision.

Men and women *should* have "butterflies" on their wedding days. They are making major decisions, many of them at a time when they know so little about themselves. Can we wonder that many marriages fail when couples decide between the ages of seventeen and twenty-four with whom they may share a life-long adventure? Is a man prepared to make that decision at that age? The answer is usually no. How can he cope with the question of marriage ability?

KNOW YOURSELF AND YOUR NEEDS

When is a man ready for marriage? I dare not suggest an all-inclusive answer to the question.

However, some points to ponder before that decision may be in order.

By using the biblical story of creation, we can gain insights about when a man is ready for marriage. Adam needed time to know himself, then time to know his needs, and time to accept Eve. To apply these to modern man requires some imagination but it can be done. Let's try.

You are only ready to marry when you know who you are. That's a major requirement, but I want to soften it in two ways. No man ever fully knows *all* about himself if he is growing; obviously there is going to be more that he will know as he grows into that self-knowledge. The basic self-knowledge that prepares us for marriage is the elemental personal awareness. It begins with setting aside the fear of self-discovery and realistically beginning to assess my own strengths and weaknesses.

The men I see who have decided to divorce their wives are often those who do not yet know themselves. Sometimes they believe a divorce is necessary because of what they have come to know about themselves. They now see themselves as incompatible with the expectations that they brought into the relationship with their present marital partner. Marriage involves basic adjustment and much compromise. The clearer your picture of yourself is the better your opportunity to adjust to marriage. To know yourself is a complex process, but there are some historical guidelines found in the disciplines of philosophy, psychology, and sociology. You can begin to know yourself by examining your thoughts, feelings, actions, and interactions with others.

One of the best ways to do this is to get input from others. Discuss with some happily married people as well as some who are divorced what they see as being keys to the successes and failures of their relationships. Listen to their ideas and share your views. You will often learn what you really think and feel as you put your thinking into words. Read books—some by male and some by female authors.

As you raise questions, react to what you hear and read, and express your ideas, you will come to know yourself. Break down the things that you learn about yourself into the categories of intellectual ideas, emotional feelings, and discipline or decision-making processes. The intellectual aspects of you take on conceptual or theoretical form. They will usually follow most easily the phrase "I think. . . ." I *think* in facts, ideas, opinions, and data. I *feel* in emotional terms that have validity, but which often defy factual data or conceptual containment. I *behave* through a combination of my thoughts and feelings in which I choose to act or react in certain ways. To some degree, all behavior is selected, established, and maintained by my will. In choosing a marriage partner, therefore, I need to examine carefully the data that I am feeding to my will about that decision.

Particularly note your strengths and weaknesses as you consider a specific woman for your life. What are your needs? Do the two of you complement each other, or are you both similar in temperament? Quite often in premarital counseling I use a testing instrument called the Taylor-Johnson Temperament Analysis as a way of helping perspective marriage partners see how they view each other. Many counselors and ministers are prepared to help a couple prior to engagement to consider these questions. Premarital counseling with your intended mate is a tremendous investment in the potential future marriage. Time is on your side—use it well! Utilize all the resources available to you as an individual and as a couple.

Probably every bride and bridegroom have some doubts on their wedding day and afterwards. Time is the only healer of those doubts. As you share a loving relationship, assurance grows and marital love deepens. For me, there was a sense of divine guidance in choosing a marriage partner. As surely as Eve came from the hand of God to Adam, a man may ask God for help in his search for a wife. This prayer-poem by a high school girl says it well:

> Dear wise and loving God above,
> Show me the girl that I should love.
> May she be good and kind and true.
> May she have faith and believe in You.
>
> Grant her a smile for each tomorrow.
> May she have wisdom and joy and sorrow.
> Let her have faults, dear Lord, you see
> I don't want her too much better than me.
>
> May she be steady, firm and sure
> That the hardships of life she may endure;
> But this, above all, dear Lord, I ask—
> As I give You this task;
>
> First, dear Lord, she must love You
> And then, may she find she loves me.

When a man discovers the love of a woman who will share his life, there is no more surpassing joy for him. He is no longer alone to face life. His rewards, shared with her, multiply, and his sorrows, lightened by her concern, divide. Depending upon the level of your spiritual development, you may sense an awareness of God's leading you to a special girl for your life. If you don't feel particularly spiritually attuned, the period of your engagement may be a good time to begin your inner journey together. Marriage is so important; you can use all the help you can get.

But don't forget my friend, Bob; he wanted to know if *this* girl was the one who would share his life, double his happiness, and divide his sorrows. I didn't know. How could he decide?

STOP, LOOK, AND LISTEN

The old adage gives one way to find out if your girl is the right one. "Look at her mother!" That's not bad advice. Although she may have other people who have helpfully or destructively influenced her, looking at your potential mother-in-law will give you a pretty good idea about the strong influences in your chosen one's life. She is more likely to either model the behavior of her mother or to rebel against the model her mother has provided.

I asked Bob four questions: Who have you known before like her? What are her basic personality characteristics? How does she handle stress situations? What are her goals for the future? Try them on for size in your life.

Who have you known before like her?

This question is directed at your understanding of the relationship to your own mother. The more the woman you choose is like your mother, beware! Unresolved dependency may be hidden like a landmine in your marital path. There may also loom a power struggle where your maternal rebellions can be extended. Without over-analyzing, the biggest problem in choosing a woman like your mother may be your relationship to your father. You may really be living out what you need to tell him about your observations of his way of relating to your own mother. He's already had a chance to live his life; don't try to correct his mistakes in your life. Be thorough in exploring this question—you may avoid much future grief.

What are her basic personality characteristics? Answering this question is vital. Is she an open person? Do you feel relaxed around her? Is she easy to be with over an extended period of time? Does she "wear well" in a relationship; that is, do you like her more as you know more about her? If she is introverted and responds only to your direct questions, there will probably come a time when you will feel very isolated from her in marriage. If you see her as needing to be "handled with kid gloves," you had better try on those gloves for size. If you don't like the fit, get out of the store! A good rule is that you won't change her after you are married. So, don't overlook what could be a source of infection to the relationship. Surgery is always possible to relieve the pressure of that infection, but it brings its own pain. Preventive action is preferable to repair work in all health fields, including marital health!

How does she handle stress? She may handle it well and that can threaten your male ego. She may "fall apart" when she doesn't get her way. She may be an "escape artist"—avoiding any unpleasant reality by running away. Failure to face up to situations can be seen in stoic denial and habitual reflexes, such as the excessive use of alcohol, cigarettes, pills, among others, or in literal physical movements away from sources of stress. Running from her family to you is probably an avoidance pattern—so stop, look, and listen! If she is extremely critical of her parents and acquaintances, how long do you think it will be until you join her disapproval list?

Finally, *compare your life goals.* If you like to roam, does she? Wanderlust turns to resentment when you feel she is "holding you back" particularly if your career is involved. Has she planned for several children while you don't really want them? Is the style of life you plan to offer one she can find acceptable for the future? Look into the mirror of the future and imagine what life with her would be like five or ten years from now. If you are not satisfied with what you see, apply the brakes now.

Love alone won't conquer *all* things. Marriage is a cooperative effort. It is not fulfilled by two people continually gazing into each other's eyes—though romance continues; rather, it is two standing shoulder to shoulder looking ahead toward the same goals. To attain those goals, you must work together. And you can only work together to attain those goals that you can both see. If this chapter troubles you, go slowly in your commitments to marriage.

Assuming marriage as the best context for the development of genuine intimacy, let's explore the different levels of male-female relationships.

CHAPTER ELEVEN

Beyond the Limits

"Peace of mind is not needing to know what is going to happen next."

—*Anonymous*

Like a good diver, the searcher in the world of intimacy must be oriented first to the differences between outer space and inner space. Just as the diver requires equipment to adequately cope with underwater pressure, so a special sensitivity is required to move successfully in the intimate world.

Let's talk about acclimatization. The delicate atmosphere of intimacy is sustained by the rare oxygen of risk to the self. Becoming fully or even partially naked to another human being requires almost superhuman courage. What seduces us into this venture is the promise of reward when our risk produces that unique sense of acceptance by another human being. Nothing quite dispels our deep feeling of being isolated like the comfort of having another person genuinely and caringly "hearing" us. Acceptance nourishes the soul and strengthens our resolve to risk again . . . and to risk more deeply.

Experiencing a rewarding risk is like eating one potato chip. You always come back for more. One must be aware of this demand if he would enjoy a satisfying intimate exchange with another. The experience of intimacy can be overwhelming and draining. Some have likened it to a step into a deep well. The sense of time and other responsibilities can be momentarily lost.

George sat across the table from me after a day-long personal growth group. As he waited for the meal he had ordered, he became aware of a new kind of exhaustion. His body, as he put it, "is fine, but I feel like my guts have been wrung out and replaced today." Something unusual for him took place in his emotional world—much like an internal wrenching! He had experienced an intensity to which he was not accustomed. Like the "second wind" of the long-distance runner, there waits to be tapped within us a reservoir of stabilizing depth. Yet we are so unaccustomed to drawing on our inner resources that few of us learn to mobilize them effectively. When disciplined, this emotional intensity heightens our awareness usefully. When it is unchecked, we experience emotional burnout. It can be a welcome friend or a devastating foe. Like fire this intensity can consume rapidly, but when controlled its glow may provide warmth and protection from the chill of human isolation.

Experiencing intimacy—knowing another person in some depth, and being known—assures us of the control and use of our emotional power. To be comfortable and basically aware of one's own inner being provides the anchor from which to explore the deeper cover of another's life. But many men are far behind women in their handling of emotional intimacy.

It is true that many of us men were taught in the socializing process that emotions were for women while logic belonged to the male domain. Subtly, and often not so subtly, women are taught in adolescence to control the emotional climate, while "boys will be boys." In more recent times women have refused to accept this responsibility alone. This change should allow for a more balanced interchange in relationships.

I want to examine fully masculine attitudes about feminine sexual responses in the next chapter. For now, the emphasis is on this fact—a woman is much more than a body.

Please don't misunderstand! Males respond to the female body, and I champion that natural biological response. However, the intimate relationships that set us above other animals operate on levels far more intricate and powerful than the physical.

Men need to move beyond the limits of socialization and past experiences to accept women in more realistic ways.

BEYOND MOTHER

A man's first relationship with a woman begins in her womb, and some men never get unattached from this protective or *maternal* view of women. If a man wants to be "mothered" all of his life, all he really has to do is play helpless. He can act like a child even if he no longer looks like a child. Usually some woman will volunteer to take care of him. There are enough maternal women in our world that almost every man can survive, even if he has to change "mothers" a few times in his life. Women provide protection for men in their early years, but unless a man moves outside the world of protection in relationship to a woman he is only "part-man." He is still a child-man, afraid to enter into the full world of reality.

Fred was a "child-man" when I met him. He held a position of authority and boasted of his awareness of himself. In each crisis of life, however, he sought a woman to protect him. When the crisis passed, and he no longer needed to lean on her, he discarded her by attacking her virtue, faithfulness, or demands on him. He was a woman-hater! "They're all alike," he said. "If they gain control, they will take you to the cleaners."

Fred taught me that men who constantly fight for control of women fear their own dependence on women. Fred could not be held responsible for his mother's influence on him, but he seemed to be controlled by it. She had regularly invited him to "return to the womb" by coming home when a crisis arose in his life. When he felt "safe," the same uneasy independence led him out into the world to "free himself." Each marriage failed because he found her! When he began to see how he was responding to his mother's influence he finally accepted responsibility for himself and became a man. I hope the process is still going on. "Momism" is a crippling disease. A man who has it needs to cut the umbilical cord before it strangles him. If your "woman's world" is predominantly a safe haven, it's time to grow up!

BEYOND PLAYMATE

Another segment of our relationship to women comes when we reach the *adult-adult* level. Here there is a new give-and-take experience of equality that causes some men to stumble. Some men get fixated into the playboy category and see women only as sexual objects for the satisfaction of their physical urges or as the satisfier of such emotional needs as prowess and conquest. If a man gets hung up at this point, then he never really knows the joy of sharing with a woman. He certainly cannot make a commitment to her, and his real relationships in life will be those he has with *men* to whom he can talk about his conquests and not with the women on whom he may indulge his ego or perpetrate his masculinity. This is a blatant form of homosexuality at the emotional level. Any man who becomes fixated at this level of functioning needs to reexamine for himself what the meaning of this behavior is.

Ed was a "super jock." He had lettered in four sports ten years ago, but he still regularly exercised and was an avid tennis and golf player. If he could have shared this with his wife and children, he might have had some great family experiences. He was shattered by his wife's affair with an "inferior" man when he came to see me.

As we dug into Ed's past together, he made some interesting discoveries! He found, as he examined his behavior, that he entered his wife's world only as a sexual performer. He learned also that his self-esteem was built on competition with men and their admiration for his athletic and business prowess.

In a group experience he found that women could respond to his feelings. He translated that insight into a new behavior with his wife. Before long he and his wife were struggling to live in an adult world instead of a protracted teen-age syndrome.

BEYOND CHAUVINISM

The third level of functioning in relationship to women comes when a man enters into the *protective* role. When he has a little girl of his own, he plays the role of father. There is a special kind of response in the heart of a man to his own daughter. Some men, however, treat all women as though they were little girls. They don't have to enter into the world of physical fatherhood in order to experience these kinds of relationships.

Much "male chauvinism" is perpetrated on women by men functioning in this way. Of course, it is enhanced by the women who enjoy being protected.

George was a real southern gentleman. He called most women "honey," and his wife seemed to like his style. When I met him he was in his third affair with a "baby doll" secretary. Because he saw himself as the great father figure he had become vulnerable. As "father," he should be able to meet any need his "girl" had. If she was not being loved by her husband, he should make sure she felt love. If she needed money, she should get it. The story could go on, ad nauseam. George was prey to his own "god" complex. He had to prove himself "the all-sufficient Daddy." He really made a mess of his life, and in the long run would not face change.

The protective male also sets himself up to get steamrolled by the rebellious liberationist! She will nail his hide to the cross, and he will protest his innocence—a game many women and men are playing today.

One of the characteristics of physical fatherhood is its changing dimensions. Fathers are seen as immensely dependable by their own daughters and give them a special security in which to grow up. As a daughter matures, she depends less on her father and more on herself. The more rebellious she is, the more she radiates her discomfort in the shift from dependence to independence. Conversely the more protective he is the more he reflects his insecurity with the changing role of his daughter. A man with a poor transition experience with his own mother is likely to experience problems with all women, particularly his wife and daughter.

OTHER WOMEN IN YOUR LIFE

Every man has decisions to make about how he is going to relate to other women in his life—those who are not his mother, his wife, or his daughter—the *other* part of the female world. A man needs to learn to relate to other women at the emotional, physical, and spiritual levels of his life.

Bankers use five words that start with the letter "c" to evaluate loans—character, capacity, capital, collateral, and condition. It dawned on me recently that these factors determine the way we relate to women.

A man's *character* defines the integrity of his relationships with women. A woman cannot trust a man who does not trust himself. If he asks her in covert or open ways to take responsibility for their relationship, he will manipulate her for his own gain. He has a poor male-female relationship character.

A man's *capacity* defines the limits of his relations to women. If he is able to perceive only the physical world, he will relate to women only as bodies. If he perceives the emotional level, he relates to women as interesting and exciting persons from whom he can learn. If he touches the spiritual, or depth core of life, he will trust and be trusted by women.

A man who knows his own capacity will negotiate openly with all the women in his life about their expectations of him and his of them. One of the marks of mature capacity is the ability to affirm a woman without being manipulatively seductive. Women trust a man like that; he feels comfortable with women.

A man's *capital* determines the depth of his relationships. In business the capital is a major determinant of the strength of the corporation. So it is in man-woman relationships. A man who knows little of himself has less to offer a woman than a man who is familiar with his body, his personality, and his spirit. Persons who complain of "outgrowing" their spouses have not really been surprised. A person's growth is dependent on the real investment of himself that he makes. The more he discloses to others, the more he knows himself. A man who is a poor communicator of himself, verbally and/or nonverbally, is a bad risk in a marriage. He has already said by implication that his investment, or commitment, to the relationship is shallow, and where his *"capital,"* his personhood is committed, his performance will follow. A committed man is going to show his beloved how he feels in his behavior and in his words. Jesus put it, "Where a man's riches are, there is his heart too."

A man's *collateral* determines his style of relating to women. He offers "real equity" in return for what he expects. What Jackson and Lederer describe in *The Mirages of Marriage* as "the quid pro quo" of a relationship is the "give and get" balance. How a man relates to his wife, his daughter, his mother, or any other woman is determined by a kind of balance sheet—what a man sees he is asked to give as compared to what he gets from their relationship. A father who invests more energy, time, and money in his daughter than in his wife is "broadcasting" his feelings about what he is getting from the two relationships.

Finally, a man's *condition* is the measure of his present awareness of how he relates to others. In business the condition of the economy may devalue certain investments and add value to the standing of others. A man who is sensitive to his daily behavior and the corresponding responses he gets is on top of his relationships. When he gets out of touch with where he is in relation to others, he is in need of updating his emotional condition.

To summarize these parallels, a man's relationship to all the women in his life is based on a broad examination of internal feelings, his past performances, his present commitments, the way he negotiates, and his ability to assess his immediate reaction.

A man is who he is, not on the basis of delegated authority from a woman or of imagined responsibility for a woman. He is a maturing man as he risks knowing himself, as he trusts himself in relation to others, and as he willingly grants others the same freedom to be what he wants for himself. Being *that* man, he will fill any woman's world with an unending challenge and the exciting reward of an unlimited relationship.

CHAPTER TWELVE

Intimacy and Intercourse

*I love you, not only for what you have made of yourself but
for what you are making of me.*
*I love you because you have done more than any creed to
make me happy.*
*You have done it without a word, without a touch,
without a sign,*
You have done it just by being yourself.
After all, perhaps that is what love is.

—*Anonymous*

THE KEYS TO HER PHYSICAL KINGDOM

Once you were expelled from the inner world of a
woman—when you were born. For many men,
life's mission seems to be to regain entry to her
magic kingdom; for others the world of women is as
threatening and mysterious as the birth process
itself. Intercourse assures physical union with a
woman. But real intimacy will not be satisfied if

limited only to her body. The intimate man's quest is to enter her mind and soul too. And beyond this desire to know the special woman in his life through full intimacy, lies the secret passion of his heart: to be known by her. What distinguishes the unexpressive from the intimate man is self-revelation. Passivity—the withdrawal of my vulnerability—protects me from risk in my encounter with the women in my life. Self-disclosure invites her to reveal herself to me.

In this chapter I want to explore the physical aspects of intimacy with a focus on lovemaking as a key. How a man creates an atmosphere of intimacy involves far more than seduction techniques.

The traditional view used to be that sex was a male domain. The stereotyped "nice" woman was not openly interested in sex. Today women are becoming more aggressive about their sexual needs, and their tolerance for lack of knowledge or poor male performance has decreased markedly. In recent years I have seen an increasing number of husbands whose wives either manipulated or dragged them into my office to talk about sexual problems. With greater awareness about sexuality, and specifically with the advent of the liberation movement, women have been demanding more fulfillment of their sexual needs. Since the sexual revolution began and the Masters and Johnson findings enlightened the public, some men have discovered that women can express themselves sexually rather exquisitely. Other men are intimidated by this knowledge. Often a man becomes temporarily or occasionally impotent as a result of greater sexual demands by his female partner. The result is an increase in the number of cases of primary and secondary impotence treated by doctors and therapists.

Let me define my terms here. Primary impotence is the inability of the man to achieve an erection; secondary impotence is the inability to achieve or maintain erection to a point where he or his female partner is able to gain satisfaction from the sexual experience they share. With this definition, of course, I include premature ejaculation as a part of secondary impotence. The premature ejaculation of the semen and sperm into the vagina is a failure or an inadequacy on the part of the man to bring sexual satisfaction to the woman.

MINDS MOTIVATE MATTER

Any man—whether or not he has experienced impotence, should first consider this: the most important gift that a man has to offer a woman sexually is not his penis. It transcends his knowledge of her anatomy. *The most important part of himself that a man can give a woman is his mind.* The sexually stimulating man first and foremost thinks about the woman in his life sensually. The "Don Juan" or "Cassanova" has been the man who is able to make a woman feel that, while with her, she is the only woman in the world.

To create that special feeling begins with how you think, what you expect, what you sense about her and how you hear her—actually how you project your thoughts about her. All of that is "mind" sexuality! Concentrate on the woman in your life. When you are critical or express your disappointment toward her, your own libido is less active. Viewing her as less than attractive will make it very difficult for you to be a sexually adequate and stimulating male. The beginning point of the "turn on" in the woman in your life is between your ears, not between your legs. What you think about her, how you feel about her, and the way you communicate that to her starts the process.

Norris was involved in an affair. His wife was not aware. Discussing affairs is not unusual, but this particular man said to me, "She is so different. My wife is inhibited. This woman is sexually liberated. My wife has an average body. The woman I'm having an affair with has an exquisite body. My wife is a good mother, but the woman that I'm having an affair with is an excellent mother: she takes care of her children, etc." He described the way "the other woman" responded to him sexually and the difference in his life since he had met her. "Have you looked at your thinking?" I asked him. He *expected* her to be this excellent person. He *expected* her to be exquisite and to be an amorous partner in bed. In many ways she was simply living up to his expectations. I suggested that before he concluded that there was no hope for the relationship he had with his wife and decided to end his marriage, he might first examine his expectations of his wife.

An interesting thing happened. When Norris began to see the reasoning I was suggesting, he made a temporary commitment that he would do the best he could to expect from his wife the kinds of things he had been experiencing with the woman of his affair.

An amazing transformation occurred. The next time he came into my office, he said things were changing in the marriage; his wife who had been described as sexually inhibited was becoming a sexual tiger in bed! Something was happening to her. But, actually the "something" was in *his* mind. He was expecting her to be more adequate, more sexual during this time of new commitment in his life. She was living up to his expectations!

I am not suggesting in every situation where a husband or wife is having an affair that all it takes is for one of them to think differently about their relationship to make a change. But, if people will begin to *think* differently about each other, the *behavior* they share will change greatly. The mind instigates the movements.

TALK TO HER

To think expectantly about the woman in your life is insufficient. The world is full of great poets who never got the words out of their minds—so we don't know who they are. Many unpublished novels were never put on paper. The second gift a man offers a woman, to be a sexually adequate male, is his *mouth*!

His mouth as an instrument of verbal communication *tells* her how he feels, what's happening in his head, his expectations of her, what he admires, and what he experiences in their relationships. Words are vital. A major complaint I hear from women is that men rarely say, "I love you," unless they desire intercourse. "He never tells me I'm pretty unless he is ready for us to go to bed." "He never says I'm attractive unless he's got that gleam in his eyes, and I know what that means." Sound familiar?

Share with the woman in your life what you are thinking about her and about life. Being a sexually adequate male involves communicating lovingly with her. Open up your inner world to let her know your personal space. Let her become a mental astronaut, orbiting your world, breaking through into the spacious areas where you have allowed no one else to go. Where your defenses have been, invite her; share with her who you really are. You will be surprised at the closeness that results between you. Don't be satisfied to just use accurate words, which your matter-of-fact tone belies. That will only confuse her. Get in touch with your own feelings and then tell her about them clearly, with emotion, depth, and dignity. Don't expect her to be a mind reader; tell her how you feel about her—with feeling! All oratory seems less important than hearing you say, "I love you."

THE MOUTH MAKES MUSIC

The mouth is also important as a special instrument of lovemaking. Kissing and caressing her body with your mouth is a tender and gentle way of expressing your feelings about your wife. Women who are sexually dissatisfied frequently say: "He doesn't enjoy kissing me. It is just a peck on the cheek. I miss the passionate embraces and lingering kisses. I want some of the deep, probing kissing we had in our courtship." The kiss symbolizes a special form of intimacy, particularly the deep, passionate kiss. A man needs to be sensitized to the needs of the woman in his life as fully as he is to his own needs. Learn to express your feelings gently and tenderly with your lips. Use them as an erotic sensitizer of other parts of her body.

Many nonorgasmic women discover their first sexual climax through oral stimulation. It is essential then for a man to be willing to stimulate his wife's body with his mouth in order for her to gain total sexual pleasure and for him to be an adequate sexual partner. Before you decide mouth stimulation is not for you, remember that your earliest contacts with a woman's body were oral. A special sense of well-being for many women comes through having their breasts kissed and sucked, though it does not hold true for all women. Nor will all appreciate other oral contacts. But if the woman in your life has her sexual motor put into high gear by oral contact, you will miss some fantastic responses by failing to give her this pleasure. Offer her your mouth for her enjoyment—she will let you know her limits. Her fulfillment is your goal; the greatest lover never loses sight of his beloved's needs.

THE GIFT OF YOUR HANDS

The third major piece of equipment for the sexually adequate male is his *hands*. Many sexual therapy programs begin with the use of massage. Sensory awareness experiences, in which couples are asked to touch each other, are ways of encouraging them to talk about their feelings. Too often we eliminate touch in our relationships apart from intercourse. How long has it been since you gave your wife a massage, starting with her head and massaging her body all the way down to her toes, front and back? You may communicate more appreciation and sensitivity through your hands than you realize. I ask husbands and wives to use their hands in becoming sensitized to feelings and needs for each other—gentle finger tapping, gentle touching of the fingertips on the face and the rest of the body in sensual exercise.

Ron and Freda had great difficulty in communicating both verbally and sexually when we met. In our fifth session I asked them to face each other and hold hands as they tried to talk. When they concluded the exercise, turning toward me the hands were still clasped. Freda said, "I haven't felt this close to Ron in a long time." Together they practiced touching each other. A new intimacy developed and in time their sexual relationship improved. Touching provided a genuine testing moment in their communication. Eventually that physical contact supported changes in their love-making. What they discovered was the importance of their hands in the communication process.

The intimate man not only recognizes the value of his touch but he uses it regularly and effectively. Long before there is a genital union of bodies he begins an intricate and sensitive concert of skillful touch to create a climate of responsiveness deep within her. His hands are an essential prelude to intercourse.

The sexually adequate man, in my judgment, is not penis-centered. Many men in our society are self-centered and, to put it in the vernacular, "hung up" about the size of their penises or how they can function sexually. As I see it, a competent male could function even if he were missing his penis because of the importance of the other three gifts he has to give a woman—his mind, his mouth, and his hands. A number of veterans' wives have confirmed this fact, continuing happy, sexually fulfilling relationships even though their husbands were completely paralyzed from the waist down. Loving expressions, feelings, and sharing with each other as you grow older in your marital life need not be curtailed because of the decreasing ability to function sexually, which occurs in some (though not all) men.

INTIMACY GROWS

The sexual experience between a man and a woman is the highest form of physical intimacy that the human being can know. A whole man uses the totality of what he knows about himself to seek more adequate and rewarding experiences in sex, just as he does about other aspects of life. Here are some suggestions for you to build a more sexually adequate relationship with your partner.

First, a fulfilling sexual relationship must be based on *empathy*—being sensitive to her needs, her feelings, and her desires. A TV commercial asks, "Want him to be more of a man? Try being more of a woman!" The opposite also holds true. Remember, the more you are aware of the needs of your sexual partner, the more you empathize with her feelings, the more you remind her and help her to feel that she is a special woman, the more you are going to feel happy and fulfilled as a man. You will experience more of the satisfaction you want in your relationship. Strengthen that relationship by communicating that empathy, by sharing your feelings with her. A growing sexual life builds on relationship-centered motivation as compared to a self-centered one. A growing relationship is reflected in mutual giving and receiving.

A positive sexual relationship is based on *self-governorship*—the capacity of each person in the relationship to govern his and her own actions in the interest of their relationship. To please your sexual partner is not to placate her. Significant is the ability to feel a sense of *identification* and *love* for your partner in the relationship.

Also important for a growing sexual relationship is a *freedom of expression*. Never compromise honest expressions of feelings. Genuine communication will be lovingly reflected in your sexual relationship. All inhibiting taboos need to be dealt with and handled in an open way. Loving honesty is always the best policy.

MAKING CHANGES

If you are not satisfied with where you are in the relationship that you share with the woman in your life, first *take stock of yourself*. List on a piece of paper (1) "What am I pleased with in our relationship?" and (2) "What parts do I want to change?" Write down the things that you are thinking so that you can look at them and, in a healthy way, "talk back" to yourself. Then sit down with that woman in your life and tell her about your feelings, frustrations, fears, and anxieties. Express appreciation to her for the ways that she has been patient with you, if that is applicable. Begin to communicate with her what your hopes are for the relationship. If this attempt toward a better sexual relationship fails and if the two of you want to communicate more effectively, don't be afraid to seek professional help. Today appropriate professionals are available in the area of sexual therapy. *Happy Loving!

*Referrals for therapists are available from the national office of the American Association for Marriage and Family Therapy, 1717 K St. N W #407 Washington, D. C. 20006. Beware of dealing with a person who is not well trained and certified by an appropriate professional organization.

PART III

Intimacy in the Changing World

"He who is not busy being born is busy dying."

Bob Dylan

CHAPTER THIRTEEN

Rookie of the Year

*"If you give a man a fish, you feed him for a day.
If you teach a man how to fish, you feed him for life."*
—Chinese Proverb

One of the places I lived as a boy was Florida. Near Clearwater, the New York Yankees, the Philadelphia Phillies, and several other major league baseball teams had winter training camps. I remember as a youngster seeing Babe Ruth, after his playing days, sitting in the stands watching the younger players and commenting on their potential and possibilities for the future. It was always a thrill for me to meet a new, young ball player in the winter league training camp and then to discover at the conclusion of his first season he was being considered for the title Rookie of the Year!

It occurs to me that almost every year of my life I have in some ways felt like a "rookie." As a little guy I was learning how to relate to my world. Next I learned how to relate to the educational system, a new grade every year; after that the socialization and courtship systems; then the world of college and vocational choices. That step leads to initial jobs, marriage, fatherhood! One has barely gotten adjusted to and comfortable with one step when another step is required. And at almost every level there is really no adequate way of preparing for the next level at which we are asked to perform. In some ways we can never stop being rookies!

A rookie's major problem is survival. He doesn't have the secure place on the team, and he must constantly hustle if he is going to keep his position or earn a starting position in the lineup. Much of the pressure that a man feels in his life is like that of being a rookie; he is constantly working to survive.

SURVIVAL AND MEANING

Some years ago I read a study of churches in the San Francisco Bay area. I was impressed by the author's description of institutions going through two stages—the *survival* stage and the *meaning* stage. When you're struggling for survival, it's very difficult to ask questions about meaning.

When a man marries, he may have his mind made up to be the Rookie of the Year as a marriage partner. His attempt will probably last well through the honeymoon and into the first year of the marriage. He soon discovers, as does his wife, the demands they must meet to survive in the wonderful world of newlywed bliss! Too often the young husband becomes bogged down in making a living or, perhaps even worse, his career begins to skyrocket and he becomes absorbed in each new success. He may truly be a sensational young man on his company scene, but it may be that this success causes great failure—the relationship with his wife.

He becomes preoccupied with his need to survive at the next management level, and he moves up quickly. The old adage "success breeds success" is probably true, but it often can create chasms in relationships. This growing distance between husband and wife may be the result of his preoccupation with his career success. He finds it so easy to justify. She will be proud of him! He wants to please her by providing her all the good things they have dreamed about together. It all happens so innocently. Now they are able to afford to have the baby. She becomes pregnant and stays home while he works long hours. The loneliness in both of them grows. He feels pressure, physical fatigue, and senses her dependence on him for some contact with the outside world. She begins to feel more restricted, less satisfied, and senses somehow that he is "slipping away" from her.

As her possessiveness increases, his defensiveness and elusiveness build. Then they begin to ask the fatal question: What does our relationship mean? By this time they have usually reached the sixth to ninth years of their marriage and the "rut" has gotten deep. Perhaps a second child is now in the picture. There is more and more necessity for "surviving" and less and less reason for asking "why." Underneath their life-style are more demands for meaning and less motivation to continue surviving without knowing the answers. Frustration sets in, and the "perfect marriage" begins to become the impossible dream.

SELF-PROTECTIVE SYSTEMS

What's happening to our Rookie of the Year? Here are examples of ways men I know cope with this crisis in their lives. First look at Joe. Joe is twenty-eight years old and a fairly successful young vice-president in his company. He has been married eight years, has two children, and the gloss of his relationship to his wife and job has really worn off.

I'll Follow You

As his mechanism of defense against this tradition period in his life Joe chooses what psychologists call *introjection*. He takes into himself the feelings and emotions of other people. The most important person whom he seeks to emulate is his boss. He becomes a great "company man." His boss wears gray suits to work; Joe wears gray suits to work. His boss joins the country club; Joe joins the country club. His boss drinks; Joe drinks. His boss acts nonchalant about his relationship to his wife and Joe acts nonchalant in his relationship to his wife. Joe almost becomes a carbon copy of the person son he is using as a pattern for his life. This is introjection.

He may also emulate his wife! Some couples become so much alike that it's hard to tell them apart. The "similarity" marriage is two people agreeing on everything. A carbon copy really adds nothing to the original; it only reminds us of what the original was. One partner becomes unnecessary. When another person patterns his life after his partner, his boss, or any other individual, to the point that he has nothing left that is uniquely his own, then his life is really a waste—unnecessary.

Everything Is Beautiful

Let's look at Frank. Frank is a *denier*. He pretends that everything is great in his life. He pretends there is no question of survival; there has been no survival period; there is no quest for "meaning" in his life. He and his wife have been married for twelve years. They have *never* had a fuss or a fight, and everything is wonderful; but Frank is denying reality. His denial may show up somatically—perhaps an ulcer, migraine headaches, or in some other physical symptom.

Frank's need to keep himself charged up under these circumstances will become even greater. As a defense he will find himself needing to invest in causes and circumstances that prove everything is not like his "gut" tells him it is. He gets busy; he works hard. He does all the things he is supposed to do, becoming a tremendous achiever. But achieving doesn't answer his questions.

"It's Later Than I Thought"

Another kind of defense in which a man may engage is what psychologists call *regression*. He may revert to a previous level of functioning, which is less than his normal behavior. He finds a new romance in his life, which *could* mean he falls in love again with his wife, or it could mean he has an affair with another woman!

It could mean that he starts to "play." Very often when a man goes through what Edmund Bergler called "the revolt of the middle-aged man," he is regressing to an earlier period of living. He is a teen-ager again! He buys a red convertible. He adds some flashy new clothes to his wardrobe. He changes his hairstyle. He loses weight and seeks to change his physical appearance. All of this, which sometimes appears to be a way of "regaining his youth," is a regression back to an earlier period of behavior. He uses this "second time around" to defend himself against the crisis in his life—aging. The fear of growing older pushes him back toward childhood.

"I Need a New Challenge"

Another form of defense is *escapism*. Jack, at twenty-nine had succeeded at being "Rookie of the Year," but he could sense that his days of being the new boy on the block were numbered. He transferred to a new level and tried to become the "sophomore sensation" in his line of business. He could have attempted escape by changing his vocation, by the use of alcohol or drugs, or developing another relationship. He might try to escape by burying himself in his work. In any case he is trying to run away from his feelings by escaping from the consequences of what he is do- ing. At best he postpones those consequences, but he never avoids them. Only the irrational believes it is better to escape than to face life's difficulties and one's responsibilities.

Comfortable Digression

A painful form of defense is *fixation*. This idea has been popularized by books such as *The Peter Principle*. One can defend oneself against any crisis by simply staying at the level at which one has become comfortable. A man becomes a robot! He may function well, but there is no way up and very little way back in his life. This often leads to severe depression. Harold worked for a company in which he had achieved a certain level of expertise. There was no way for him to go higher in the company, as he saw it, but he had excellent job security. Then an awful depression hit him! He soon began to see that it was a result of his being fixated or trapped. His depression grew. When he finally came to me for help, before he could make any progress he had to give up the security of the comfortable level of his life to advance to a new level. When he took that risk, he broke the depressive cycle.

Perfectionist

A final picture of the defenses against life's crises brings Paul to mind. Paul is afraid of appearing "burned-out" at forty. He has experienced great success in his line of work, but he often feels there is no place to go. He works hard at appearing alive with new ideas and new opportunities, when underneath he is struggling to find any satisfaction in his present job.

He is a determined man, a perfectionist. I listened

to Paul use the word "must" nearly one hundred times in the first two hours I saw him. He used the word so often that I began to pencil out a message on my notebook paper. It became *Man Under Stress and Tension*. Then I wrote, *Man Unloading Strain and Terror*. The more I listened to the drive and the ambition in Paul, the more I heard the stress, fear, and the terror.

Failing to constantly achieve something new is the mark of the perfectionist—*the driven man*. He whips himself onward to the next level of achievement, the next goal. He has within himself an "insistent" parent (to use a transactional analysis term). Only what he fails to do has significance—what he has already accomplished fades quickly. Compulsively, he drives even harder toward the next project or challenge. But, sadly, he has no time to enjoy what he has achieved. He urges others to move ahead. He is annoyed by the relaxation of others.

FEAR OF THE UNKNOWN

The specific threat of being a man in the woman's world of today is the challenge of *old expectations*. The liberation movement has caused us to ask, "What are the things that 'men should do' and 'women should do'?" Some men are terribly threatened by the fall of "protected sanctuaries" like bars, men's clubs, etc. Other men are troubled by vocational assertiveness on the part of women who are taking over the jobs they feel "only a man can do." To deal with this fear in himself, a man must ask himself, "Where does real security lie? Is it in what I do or is it in who I am?"

I strongly suggest that *who* a man is determines *what* he does. The same holds true for a woman. If either of them needs to prove something about themselves, they will attempt to make those "brownie points"as long as they live. There will always be "male strongholds" for some women to try to overcome, and there will always be some "protected sanctuaries" for some men to guard.

In Sarah Connelly's *The Unquiet Grave* there is a line that succinctly states the issue: "two fears alternate, the one of loneliness and one other of bondage." Whenever a man protects something by a barrier against the outside world, he also limits himself to the safety behind the barrier. What I am unwilling to share with another person must be "enjoyed" in isolation!

A man who defines his world by things specifically masculine in orientation will live with a consuming fear of the female world. The converse is true for a woman. What is *different* from me has the potential of *threatening* me. Too many of us choose only to defend ourselves against the threat. We too seldom recognize the pleasure of exploring the unknown or the different in life. A man fears a woman's true self-liberation only if that freedom inherently demands too much responsibility from him.

Only the man who knows himself comfortably can ever fully know a woman. That which I fear in myself and will not accept, I will project on to another and despise.

[110]

The "Rookie" maturational period is marked by a knowledge of my strengths and my attempts to "sell" them to the world around me. As I mature in life, I am willing to face my limitations and to learn to live fully in spite of them. I don't fear my weakness when I know it better than anyone else. Maturity lessens fear and multiplies freedoms. The intimate man is becoming mature!

CHAPTER FOURTEEN

Why Men Like Women

"Why should men like women?" he asked. I viewed my young homosexual client and heard no defensiveness in his question. "I usually have difficulty liking what is *expected* of me," I responded. Our session progressed along other lines, but his query remained with me for days. Let's explore it further.

In one sense a man *should* like men not women. If identification is a primary function of psychological bonding, then a man is a more appropriate model. In a balanced development every boy needs a man with whom to identify. My young patient had lived with his mother from age two to eighteen without contact with his father or many other men. Widowed by a war death, his mother devoted herself to the children and resented her plight in life. Unintentionally she communicated her negative feelings to her son about men. They were not dependable! Obviously, her feeling of being deserted or abandoned by her young husband's death was neurotic, but she overprotected her son from harm or injury. He grew up feeling that women, like wardens, imprisoned males and stripped them of their freedom. To avoid that, he associated with the gay world where he thought the "bondage" of marriage would not engulf him. His own lover had left him, and he seemed genuinely puzzled about where his homosexual tendency might end. Could he learn to like women?

WHOLENESS

Men like women for some very natural reasons; one is *a sense of wholeness*. The sexual complement is obvious. Like pieces of an interlocking puzzle men fit women. More subtly the psychological edges of males and females are magnetized and draw toward each other in a powerful union.

In the Hebrew tradition the rabbi at a wedding says, "Woman was taken from man's rib. She was not taken from his head to rule him or from his foot to be trampled under him. She came from his side to be equal. She came from under his arm to be protected by him and from near his heart to be loved by him."

Human wholeness is more than the sum of its two complementary parts, male and female. In a unique way a man and woman can each become more together than they were alone. When male and female join to become one, ideally each is enhanced.

Bert and Nita are good illustrations. A bachelor for six years after college, he was quite capable of independent existence. When Nita married him, each of them found strengths made more obvious by their shared life. Their capability to live alone produced a sense of pleasure in choosing not to do so. Bert described it this way. "I enjoy nature. Climbing to the top of a mountain ridge to enjoy a sunset is really rewarding. I've always found great satisfaction in doing that. Now when Nita and I hike to the crest, I get more pleasure because we share the view. I'm delighted by her enthusiasm. She enriches my good times in life."

Nita viewed it in a different way. "Bert's presence is like fitting the last piece in a puzzle. The challenge is fun, but the completed project is really satisfying. Because of him, what I've done in life makes more sense. It's not that I *need* him as much as I enjoy his wanting me like I want him."

The descriptions of their sense of completion in marriage rang true as I listened. Men and women enjoy the feeling of "fitting" into each other's lives. A special sense of wholeness radiates from that kind of union.

BALANCE

Balance provides another element of male-female attraction. We like each other because we are different. A special mystery surrounds the unknown—those parts of the universe not like me. This phenomenon enhances the encounters between men and women at many levels. The physical, emotional, or spiritual sharing between members of the opposite sex has a unique quality.

I have led many different types of therapy

groups. Some have been all female; some all male. The most consistent growth comes in mixed groups. In these therapy groups it is obvious that the men not only listen rather intently to each other, but also to the women, and find that some relationships become significant. They use these opportunities to balance what they have learned about other women. For a special sense of wholeness, a unique relationship with one person of the opposite sex provides the maximum rewards. However, for balance a variety of significant persons is more useful.

Jerry can illustrate this thoroughly. He came to the personal growth group where there were four other men, including the therapist, and five women. In the course of his time in the group each of the women responded to him in a way similar to the special women in his life—his mother, his sister, his ex-wife, his daughter, and his present wife. The beauty of Jerry's learning was not so much what took place in the group sessions, but the relieving of many of his fears in dealing with women in general.

Having developed no sense of closeness to a woman outside of sexual encounters, Jerry found himself identifying all positive feelings toward women as sexual experiences. He was very nervous the first time he acknowledged these feelings in the group. He discovered, however, that he could verbalize his feelings without acting on them. After several weeks he could distinguish between the heat of sexual attraction and the warmth of openness.

"Intimacy—being close emotionally to a woman—has always been related to sex for me," he said, through tears of relief. "I'm glad to know I can have female friends I don't have to take to bed."

Jerry's story might easily have been one told by a female. The same fears dominate many women. In developing honest relationships, these fears can be reduced and sometimes eliminated entirely.

Men enjoy women because they provide a necessary balance, like a partner on the other end of a seesaw. The cooperative male-female relationship may be more socially exciting than the competitive one. Shoulder-to-shoulder sharing of tasks, insights, and feelings is preferable.

BLENDING

A step beyond the complementarity of the physical elements and the balance of the emotional ingredient is the blending of two lives—a kind of spiritual or mystical union of man and woman. Intimacy, the broad term, defines for us the sensual, verbal, psychological-emotional, and the spiritual sensitivities where men and women meet. Though multifaceted, it is all one, a continuum running from the basic spatial and physical levels to the opposite poles of mystical bonding.

Spatial or physical intimacy involves our needs for both distance and closeness. Each of us mentally erects a barrier where our comfort zones are triggered physically. Standing in the ticket line or on a crowded elevator one quickly becomes aware of his feelings about physical intimacy or closeness.

Some of us respond in ways that surprise us in these circumstances.

Daryl, a young, married, professional man, seemed extremely nervous during an office appointment. "This morning in the elevator a rather heavyset woman was in front of me. As the space became more limited she backed closer until her buttocks touched me. I got an erection. It was really embarrassing."

His involuntary response to physical contact was not the result of "lusting" after the female who stood in front of him as he had feared. We explored what physical contact meant to him. Having rarely been touched while growing up, especially by his mother—at least as he recalled his childhood—he was more uneasy about physical closeness to women than to men. His feelings about men had changed during his high school and college athletic experiences where much physical intimacy and contact was involved in a natural and less threatening way. Having dated little in college, he had been painfully shy around women. His wife of four months was the only woman with whom he had experienced intercourse. While he was becoming more comfortable in the privacy of their bedroom, he still experienced discomfort, anxiety, and frequent blushing in close physical contact with other women. Dancing with another woman, while part of his social pattern, was definitely not his favorite activity.

Tension and mild distress for people like Daryl are unpleasant relics of a childhood lacking appropriate touching and physical contact. Not everyone becomes comfortable with close physical encounters. One aspect of claustrophobia—the morbid fear of enclosed spaces—may be experienced in crowds of people. Allowing one's self the opportunities to become accustomed to physical contact begins the process of change.

Most of us, however, sense only minimal discomfort in social situations. Our more basic fears of physical intimacy show up in the relationships with friends. Men like women who blend their own self-assurance about being touched with positive responses such as smiles, other nonverbal clues or words. Women, no doubt, enjoy men who similarly reach to them.

Physical intimacy—touching—is more acceptable in its giving form at most levels of contact. A touch that pleases the individual receiving it brings not only physical pleasure but emotional comfort. The predatory "taking" touch threatens its intended victim. The "grabber" almost always repels people; the "giver" rarely does.

Verbal intimacy also frightens us until we learn its risks and rewards. Much of the exchange between people takes place at the lowest levels of risk— dealing with the weather, current events, and observable data. Little listening energy is required at that level. Such *minimum* communication is words without feelings involved. Two computers could easily make these exchanges. *Protective* communication is a message with a triple meaning. My words may be different from my feelings, but I do not acknowledge this discrepancy. Sarcasm is a good example. If you confront me with my feelings,

I can call your attention to my words. If you respond to my words, I point out that you misunderstood my feeling. I am protected by my options. *Intimate* communication reveals my authentic feelings in the most appropriate words I can find. I risk genuinely letting you know me.

The obvious place for any of us to learn this verbal openness is in the family. Failing there, the church or the school would provide logical opportunities to gain these verbal skills. College, friendships, employment, or finally the marriage relationship should enhance our possibilities of experiencing this verbal intimacy. Psychotherapy would seem to be a last resort. Unfortunately, my experience has been that therapy seems quite often to be the first verbal honesty breakthrough for many adults.

Psychological-emotional intimacy depends on relationships. A variety of facets of my personality are challenged by different kinds of encounters with males and females. Real growth progresses only with an appropriate complement of meaningful relationships. If I do not experience this diversity in people encounters, the result is emotional dullness—limited resources in responsiveness.

Recognizing that men like and need women for an infinite variety of reasons, the most common response that I hear from men can be summed up in this word—excitement. This is beyond the physical titillation level and the stimulating effect of a good conversation. At the *core of men*—and I expect it is equally true of women—*lies the need to be excitingly encountering a person of the opposite sex!* Social relationships are the blending of people attractive to each other. Emotional bonding turns on a stimulating identification or balance with another person. The marital secret of staying in love lies in the quest of fully sharing the pursuit of living together.

Male-female friendships provide a needed ingredient of emotional excitement. Healthy marriages include good friendships with other couples and individuals. A happy husband can share the positive benefits of his relationships with other women to deepen his sharing in his marriage. The man limited in his total life relationships will probably also be limited in his responding to his wife. As they learn to risk, all associations produce fuel for their relational machinery.

Intimacy needs to be pumped to the heart of the male-female connection. The importance vested in each relationship is determined by the value of the role fulfilled in the relationship. Another significant deterrent to full intimacy may appear unrelated. It is vocational stress. But that's the next chapter.

CHAPTER FIFTEEN

The Career Mid-life Crisis and Intimacy

"Whatever my secrets are, remember when I entrust them to you, they are part of me."
—John Powell

Mid-life crisis has become a familiar phrase in the last decade. Thirty percent of the cases involving marital conflict in the last fifteen years have been infected with a subtle career pressure. The symptoms sound like this.

Steve was a handsome, well-built, young professional. He looked somewhat younger than forty-four. He told me what I have come to expect from a man his age: "I'm tired of being married. I'm just not a family man. I don't love my wife. I care for her and the children. I want to do the right thing by them. I will continue to provide for them financially, but I'm in love with another woman." The elements in his story seemed familiar. When I probed further as we got to know each other, he told me he was in a family business. He enjoyed his work, but it was less challenging now. His only problem with the career was that he had become accustomed to the money. While he might enjoy a change, he could see no way to equal his present income in another field. He had lost weight within the last six months, gotten a basically new wardrobe, and met a younger, single woman. As he described her, "she's really a very sensible, level-headed Christian girl, but I've flipped over her."

Steve experienced five things common to career-marriage pressure: career success, less challenge in his vocational conquests, a sense of fatigue from pressure to keep producing at high levels, a feeling of "loss" in the marriage and family context, and some significant physical and emotional changes, including an affair. Perhaps the weakest link in his chain of defense was his vague description of family-marital dissatisfaction. The more we talked about it, the more obvious it became that the easiest changes in his life to make were in that area. He had not consciously focused on that, but he began to realize what was happening.

While not true of every mid-life crisis, these five ingredients are present in so many that they merit elaboration. The first is *career success*. Not all men have serious career problems or go through mid-life evaluations. But I do think that most men and women pass through major transitions that cause them to evaluate their life goals and commitments. I have also observed that the majority of highly successful people will tire or even burn out in twelve to seventeen years. This contributes strongly to the common experience of pulling away from a marriage described as happy or strong. After that period the yearning for a new and exciting intimate relationship is more likely to arise. The seeds of discontent in much marital disharmony are in the career or vocational arena. The first principle I use is this: change the least permanent relationship first. That usually means exploring a job change before looking at a divorce or family adjustment.

On balance some very successful types experience similar stress and must adhere to the same principle in resolving their conflicts. But after reaching the achievement for which one has struggled, like climbing a mountain top, one then often yearns for *a new challenge*. When the loss of rewards seems perilously great, then a diversionary, an apparently intimate change—such as an affair—becomes more appealing. The element of challenge, lost in the business or professional dimension, finds fulfillment in other arenas. When this is combined with the natural tendency of a husband to become career-minded and the wife to become child-oriented during this stage of their marriage, *a mid-life explosion is fueled*. While I am emphasizing here the impact on the male, very similar transitions will affect many working women —involving currently about fifty-five percent of the households in the United States.

Too often our career successes bring a certain *disillusionment*. Promotions may come too easily and even raises aren't quite as hard to get. We begin to lose the challenge. Although Steve was not in aviation, he had what I call "pilot's disease." It may well apply to other professions such as athletics, where people are paid quite well for the few visible hours they work. Very often they become bored with their lack of challenge. For a pilot, unless an emergency arises, he merely watches very sophisticated machinery do its work. I have seen many airline pilots fail at other businesses, especially those for which they were less prepared, because they were seeking new challenges. At the heart of their dissatisfaction is the need to become involved again. Their success has produced a detachment. They need to be close to the action again.

Fatigue is another major component of the critical mid-life shifts. Overworked, exhausted, and immersed in the multiple demands of life, so many men long for a few precious moments of relaxation. "I need to get away from it all some time," Steve said. "I need some time just to think, to feel what I'm all about. Everybody wants a piece of me—my boss, my secretary, my wife, my kids. There's not much left for me. I'm tired of being pulled in so many directions."

Fatigued bodies and minds often fail moral and spiritual tests they might pass if rested. Steve had. "It wasn't until I got away and rested that I saw how dumb my actions were."

Another element he experienced was a *loss of attachment* to his family. He recounted the joy he used to feel in coming home to his wife and children. "Now I feel like a pay check. As long as I pay the bills, they will get along fine." This feeling of loss of purpose in belonging is prevalent in many working men and women. We long for the closeness of feeling needed personally rather than functionally. Every person wants to feel he is more than a pay check to someone!

One final dimension of this process needs attention—the outbreak once described by Edmund Berger as "the revolt of the middle-aged man." Unfulfilled intimacy needs are closely tied to the *longings,* which burst into transitional flames.

Steve's case illustrates this point. After he turned forty, Steve began to realize that his somewhat athletic body had begun to spread near the middle. He joined a health spa and lost some weight, while toning up his muscle structure. The "new" Steve felt good and looked good. Almost everyone around him commented positively about his new look. Cheryl, his lovely and successful wife, was less adoring, occasionally even chiding him about his choice of wardrobe, which was obviously influenced by his younger spa buddies and younger business associates. She was busy with her own career, plus a seriously ill child who demanded much attention and time. By the end of the day she was ready to fall into bed, exhausted. Steve, however, began to feel the need to go out a couple of evenings a week. Since he had done this type of thing for professional reasons, Cheryl at first did not object. Then she began to resent going to bed alone and hearing him come into the house after midnight. She confronted him, and he frankly told her he no longer loved her and had discovered feelings for a girl he had met while he was out. When pressed as to the nature of the attraction, Steve admitted that the new woman in his life was less attractive than Cheryl and even less competent, but she was fun to be with and made him feel exciting with her responses.

Steve is not yet back to his senses, but he sees clearly now that the feelings he has experienced in his new relationship do not depend on the presence of "the other woman." He can enjoy the "new Steve" more, even around Cheryl, although they remain separated. Eighty-five percent of the men I have dealt with in therapy eventually restore their original relationships with their wives, some more happily and successfully than others. The restoration and renewal time usually spans six to eighteen months.

Steve's reevaluation centered around three questions he had to deal with in this order: (1) Who am I and what do I want from my life? (2) What do my answers to this question mean to my present marriage and family circumstance? (3) If my answers to question one do not involve continuing my marriage, what do they mean in relation to "x"? He found that he could not compare Cheryl to this new girl to make a decision. When he began to describe himself as a community-minded professional, a churchman, maybe a family man, his desperate frustration began to recede. The impact of the dilemma will not soon be resolved, but the urgency of decision has. Steve has given himself time to decide this important matter and Cheryl has discovered more patient understanding. They are talking and listening again.

Every man faces these transitions in his life. The growing male risks sharing his fears with someone, preferably his wife, and uses the situational stress as motivation for new levels of intimate disclosure and contact. Withdrawal and retreat are the marks of fear. The more he denies the more vulnerable he becomes to the pressure.

When you walk through this valley, take a good look at what is happening around you, find ways to verbalize your feelings, pray for strength, and discover more of the inexhaustible mystery that lies within you. Intimacy is self-rewarding. The more you know of yourself, the less you can be surprised by what others tell you. Truly you will experience inner strength and healing in intimate knowledge and self-disclosure.

PART IV

Intimacy and Reality

*"But it is not the spiritual which is first but the physical,
and then the spiritual."*

1 Corinthians 15:46 (RSV)

CHAPTER SIXTEEN

Intimacy and Aging

*"If two people who have been strangers, as all of us are,
suddenly let the wall between them break down, and feel
close, feel one, this moment of oneness is one of the most
exhilarating, most exciting experiences in life.*

—Erich Fromm, *The Art of Loving*

The maturing man may be more in tune with his
intimacy needs than a man some years his junior. In
the early years of life our insecurities can be hidden
in activity and physical prowess, but when we get
older those avenues are not so available to us. Some
men still attempt to be young and to do the things
that once characterized them. That is no doubt the
origin of the statement, "There's no fool like an old
fool."

CONFLICT IN MATURING

Men mature differently than women. In marriages of some duration, I've observed an interesting, somewhat predictable, phenomenon. As men

mature, they frequently move from the pressing external demands of their careers to a greater sense of personal and internal awareness. In the process of looking inward, they often begin to evaluate the past, occasionally finding that depressing. Sometimes they begin to desire to spend more time around the house. Frequently, they develop hobbies that were not characteristic of their more youthful years, such as gardening, reading, stamp-collecting, etc. These may allow more time for immediate reflection and quiet solitude.

Interestingly, women who have majored in homemaking make a strikingly different transition. Since the children have grown and the home where she has spent so much of her time is now less demanding, she is often ready for more activities away from the home, whether in salaried or self-employed vocational interests or more avocational and voluntary pursuits. The conflicts which may arise are obvious. Bitterness can emerge from these struggles.

When I met Mert and Edwina, their hostile vibrations were almost visible. I found them to be a rather attractive couple, both physically trim, athletic in appearance; and although appearing mature, they both had a certain anticipation about their future living. In fact that was where the conflict began. When he retired, although the company maintained an office for him to which he made daily visits, he began to spend much more time around the house. "Ed," as he called her, was used to considerably more privacy and time for planning, executing, and adjusting tasks as she chose. As he observed her styles of management, he chose to become a consultant. His advice fell not only on deaf but on resistant ears. "I wish he'd get out of here and let me do the things I'm used to doing in my own way," she bristled.

Not only was there some conflict over space and time management in the home, but also over the activities away from home. Both Mert and Ed were good golfers and enjoyed the sport. She had looked forward to traveling and being able to play golf more when he retired. They did, but Mert became quite conservative with money. Ed found it more than frustrating to be called on to account for money she had been free to spend earlier. But for her the most painful complaint was about something she could not understand. "I've always enjoyed sex; I've even been multi-orgasmic," she said, "but I find myself resisting his advances in the daylight hours. He gets mad; and when I snuggle up to him at night, he withdraws. We can go several days with this mad between us. Help!"

Timing was an apparent problem, but control was a bigger issue. Mert privately told me how disappointed he was that Ed wasn't willing to break some of the old habits and make love during the daytime. He also complained about her activities at the church and the women's club, which took her away from home and left him alone. He had been spoiled over the years by her adaptations to his schedule, and he was often pouting because he didn't get his way. At first as we confronted these issues, he became more defensive and demanding. I felt an early sense of loss of hope in the marriage.

But they stayed with the process and we found ways together to work at compromises. Mert's most important discoveries came from within himself. He had become insensitive to Ed's needs over the years. He "appreciated her," as he so often said, but his own plans came first. Time and some rather painful confrontations finally brought him to a more mutual understanding of the process of planning and decision-making within the relationship. Then, he went into a rather deep depression for several months. Guilt over his past insensitivity, his failure to be more open to his children, and the lost opportunities for developing relationships plagued him. Ed fluctuated between impatience and anxiety about him, but she really loved him and managed to endure a major overhaul in Mert's mental process. She worked through some of her own passive hostility and became much more vocal about her needs. Almost a year later they seemed ready to embark on a successful pursuit of their retirement years.

LEARNING FROM CONFLICT

Frank and Marie had less hostility but as much conflict. They were both in their mid-fifties when I met them. Frank had traveled in his business for nearly twenty years. Marie had basically stayed near the home and raised the children. When their fourth child left for college, she began a small business from her home. It surprised her by mushrooming into a much more demanding but excitingly successful thing. Soon she had a small factory for production, a mail order division, a training program she managed, and invitations to travel to market her products in other parts of the country. Her effusive personality really blossomed, and she was elated with her personal and financial success. Frank sought help because he was beginning to drink more on the road and confidentially told me that he had attempted to have an affair in a distant town but was impotent.

Parenthetically, I urged Frank not to share this knowledge with Marie. While he would have been relieved, I sensed it was not the time to rain on her parade. Frank became aware of his need for not only sexual intimacy but also for conversational and emotional depth in their marriage relationship. While they had developed some habitual patterns of emotional distancing, the basic quality of their commitment to each other emerged during our counseling sessions. Frank began to be able to verbalize his needs, even to expressing his fears about her success and the potential of losing her prime energy to the schedule and the rewards of what she was doing. He even told her that his needs would be met if she sold her business and "things got back to normal around the house." Marie didn't choose that option. Finally, they agreed on a period of adjustment to see what would happen in the businesses and the relationship. I worked with both of them individually and in groups for several months before we had more conjoint visits.

From Function to Feeling

Since the focus of this book is the intimate man, I want to concentrate on Frank's insights. There were four major movements in his year-long growth process. The first was a shift from functional to feeling focus. As he put it, "I've been so busy doing things most of my life, I just haven't taken time to know how to be me. Who I am is so much more important than what I do." Frank's real vision of this difference came as he observed Marie's success and her subsequent life changes. At first he thought that her growth was negative. He had always seen her as a feeling person. Sometimes he had thought that was a weakness in her. Then he began to recognize her emotional strengths. She enjoyed the active success that he had taken for granted, but her ideas about who she was didn't change a great deal. In their more open conversations, Frank was able to admit to her that he was more threatened by the changes going on in him than what he feared might take place in her. Their vulnerability toward each other created a new sense of intimacy in the relationship.

From Logic to Emotion

The second element in Frank's change was a shift from a logical and rational base to a more perceptive and emotional one. He had always taken pride in his ability to remain detached and logical in emotional situations. He didn't lose the strength of that objectivity, but he gained a sense of participating and sharing with Marie and with others by truly experiencing things. "I learned to be there—it's like an emotional *withness*; I know I'm feeling it, and other people hear me speak more empathetically. I'm feeling more closeness," Frank said. "When my son was fired from his job, I could feel his pain—the ache of being rejected. I think we got closer because he knew I cared about how he felt, not just whether he had enough money to survive." Frank became much more articulate over the course of his experience in a ten-week personal growth group where he focused on self-disclosure and reflective skills; but it was his risk in using these new abilities that caused the basic changes.

From Intake to Output

The third dimension of his change took place concurrently with, but not directly related to, the counseling process. I had suggested that Frank and Marie find ways to have special times for sharing with each other. One weekend they flew to southern California and stayed in a beachfront hotel. In the same facility a Faith at Work conference was in session. Marie noticed people smiling, hugging each other, and enjoying an open expression of their feelings toward each other. She approached one of the women, introduced herself, and asked about the group. The woman she met later brought her husband to meet Frank, and they became better acquainted over breakfast the next day. This couple from a midwestern small town had a tremendous influence on Frank as he saw the meaning of their personal, spiritual faith. He came home and talked to his local minister who fortunately understood some of Frank's struggle and helped him make a personal commitment of his own life to Christ. "That was when I began to learn that giving was better than getting," Frank said. "I have come to realize that my life was self-centered; it really feels good to be able to invest some concern and help in somebody else." Frank's experience of "being born again" changed his perspective from focusing on the intake of his living to the output he shared.

From Control to Support

The fourth area, which was especially helpful for his own intimate relationship, was his insight into his controlling behavior. Marie often passively resisted his controls, but she felt dominated until her business success provided new freedoms. To Frank's credit he slowly began to see his own insensitivity and began to support her growth and success rather than criticizing as he had done earlier. Marie responded almost with distrust initially, but as she began to feel secure with his new reactions, she felt more comfortable sharing things with him. From the early and more functional ideas, they began to develop deeper understanding and insight. Marie described it beautifully one day when she said: "Frank used to be the man who filled the husband's role in my life, the father of my children; now he's become not only a trusted business advisor; he's really my best friend." There was a twinkle in her eye that told me the friendship was becoming more exciting sexually as well.

Frank's story is typical. As a man ages, his needs and focus in life will change. What once highly motivated him may become far less stimulating. If he is fortunate enough to have an understanding wife, a good friend, a minister, or a professional therapist with whom he can verbally work through these transitions, then the later years may well be more rewarding than the early ones were.

For most men, though not all, accomplishments will be less central and relationships will be more important as they mature. Arvella Schuller once told her famous television preacher husband, Robert, that old men either get "twinkly" as they age or they get "crotchety." The positive and growing man has a better chance of maintaining that inner glow and excitement than does the pessimistic and belligerent man. Knowing one's own inner world and being able to share it with those closest to us as we age enhances our sense of intimacy and fulfillment.

CHAPTER SEVENTEEN

Intimacy and Spirituality

"Hope is not a dream, but a way of making dreams become reality."

—*Postor, Abbey Press*

In the final analysis the emotional home of the individual is that place where he is truly known by himself and possibly by others. He may be aware of that place being his own living soul, where he meets his God honestly, intimately.

As we have explored it, the truth is that intimacy can be a very confusing term. Finally, let's define it. Intimacy is not love, although many people genuinely recognize love clearly only when they have experienced true intimacy. Intimacy is not sexuality, though it is common for people to appreciate their own sexuality more fully when they really know genuine intimacy. Intimacy is not spirituality, although some of us may not be cognizant of eternal truths until we feel at home in the universe of which we are a part. *Intimacy is the condition from which love, relationships of deep value, sexual expression, and faith emerge.* It is the soil of living.

Too often intimacy is so linked to the physical that we limit our thinking to sexual terms and emotional infatuations. I've heard the story so many times I could almost fill in the names and give it back to my clients before they give it to me. For our purposes he's a relatively young man with a stable marriage and healthy children. He thinks he loves his wife and would describe his life as a basically happy one. He has success and enough of its trappings like homes, automobiles, memberships, etc. to substantiate his claim to happiness. He attends a conference or convention or in the process of traveling meets another woman. Initially their relationship is casual, fun and non-intentional. He then begins to find her vital, intriguing, and exciting. If he allows himself to pursue her, he rationalizes that he has never felt like this about anyone. He may or may not become sexually involved with her, but he feels like he's "in love." He has experienced intimacy and confused it with love.

To be intimate is to position one's self for loving, but not necessarily to be "in love." Intimacy is so exhilarating because it fosters honesty, awareness of one's feelings, and the climate of vulnerability in which one desires to share himself with another. In this climate one invites others to share themselves openly. From that place love can surely emerge and grow. A fresh experience of intimacy is like a glass of fine wine; it is heady stuff. There may soon be a glow within and a feeling of relaxation. The chemistry of intimacy is so akin to romance that we often confuse the two. The romantic context invites physical or sexual intimacy, but without the commitment which enhances that sexual exchange, the tender plant may be choked with guilt or overwhelmed with anxiety.

Parenthetically, let me say that sexual intimacy is not the possession of the godless of the world. I believe that sexual union and its pleasures were created by God and intended for our unspeakable joys; these relationships were not imagined on the drawing board or photography studio of a pinup magazine or in the typewriter of a romantic novel publisher. Simply because fires may burn down houses or cities when they are uncontrolled does not mean that I am willing to sacrifice the pleasure of a blaze in my own fireplace on a cold winter evening.

But just as certainly intimacy is not spirituality either. To feel close to God is a matchless experience, but an oft-abused one. The encounter described above with a woman is just as absorbing as the overwhelming religious experiences that some men have. Paul was a middle-aged man who had a good family and a loving wife. He was an executive with a west coast engineering firm. His charismatic experience turned his life upside down. He was in a church meeting, testifying almost every night. His wife finally came to me for help. I liked Paul immediately upon meeting him, but he was one of the people who had become so heavenly minded he was almost no earthly good. There was no question about the fact that something had happened to him. In our conversations there were many examinations of Scripture. When we finally discussed the fifth chapter of Ephesians, about the filling of the Holy Spirit, I carefully asked him where the first manifestation of this filling was to take place. It was evident from what we read together that the home was the testing ground. Yet Paul's "love affair" with his new gifts had created a frustration and jealousy in his wife not much different from an affair with another woman. His new sense of intimacy with God took precedence over everything else in his life.

Intimacy provides the soil where the sensual and the spiritual can be synthesized in our lives. The intimate man knows himself, his sexual partner, and his God in an eternal triangle. The balance of the elements may be the difficult part.

Let me suggest five characteristics of the mature, intimate man. These are the outgrowth of his struggle to develop balance in living.

ACCEPTANCE

First, he accepts himself and can therefore express appreciation for the others who contribute to his life. An intimate understanding of my own inner world creates a sense of curiosity about others and a desire to affirm their search for personal fullness.

COMMUNICATION

Second, the intimate man communicates more freely with others—those closer to him as well as those he may not know as well. He not only wants to share, but he makes an effort to encourage those he cares most for to share with him.

SUPPORT

Third, the intimate man strengthens relationships in his own family and in the lives of others by positive support. He BONDS people to him and encourages others in the joining together process. Life is a sharing process, a way of saying "come along with me. I have good things to share." The intimate man is like a well, giving a refreshing spring of water that refreshes and stimulates those around him.

SHARING

Fourth, he also invests himself in those for whom he cares the most. The intimate man is a proud husband, father, employer, or member. He enjoys being a contributing part of the team. He shares himself in sharing time with people and with causes he supports.

FREEDOM

Finally, he functions without leaning unnecessarily. By his modeling he encourages others around him to be creatively whole. The quality of this kind of living was caught in the inscription of a book I read some years ago. Its title and author have faded from my memory, but the words of the dedication remain: "Who, being free, frees others to be."

The ultimate extension of isolation is called hell. By contrast the ultimate intimacy is heaven. To be an intimate man is to be at home in the universe, comfortable with one's internal resources, relationships, and potential destiny. To develop that sense of living is to come to understand the promise: "I will never leave or forsake you."

Although concluding this writing, I am aware that I can barely sketch the depths of being an intimate man. Seneca once said that "men learn while they teach." And Confucius in a similar vein wrote: "Acquire new knowledge whilst thinking over the old, and you may become a teacher of others." Our patterns of isolation are so strong that we may struggle against our own fears through most of our adult lives to experience the joy of unfettered intimacy.

Yet the work of self-knowing, the reward of dropping our barriers, and the satisfaction of sharing what we know with others makes it all worthwhile. We understand more of Paul's glimpse into the future: "For now we see in a mirror dimly, but then face to face. Now I know in part; then I shall understand fully, even as I have been fully understood" (I Cor. 13:12 RSV).